"If you're a fan of *The Simpsons*, then *Collecting The Simpsons* is a must-have for your bookshelf. As the voice of Lisa Simpson, since the very beginning, I have a lot of insider information about the show, but it turns out I didn't know that much—or anything, really—about the history of *Simpsons* merchandise. Enter Warren, James and Lydia. As avid collectors, they have written a love letter to the world of *Simpsons* collectables that have been released around the world since the show began. There's so much stuff I never even saw or knew about! The photos are gorgeous, but it's the stories about what's in the photos that kept me up well past my bedtime. Welcome to the next item in your collection."

—YEARDLEY SMITH, the voice of Lisa Simpson

COLLECTING THE SIMPSONS

THE MERCHANDISE & LEGACY OF OUR FAVORITE NUCLEAR FAMILY

Warren Evans, James & Lydia Hicks

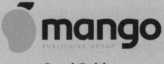

mango
PUBLISHING GROUP

Coral Gables

Cover Design: Warren Evans
Cover Photo/illustration: Caroline Walker-Evans
All photographs for chapter 13 were photographed and edited by Lydia Hicks
Interior Images: Caroline Walker-Evans
Layout & Design: Elina Diaz + Warren Evans, James & Lydia Hicks.

For permission requests, please contact the publisher at:
Mango Publishing Group
2850 S Douglas Road, 2nd Floor
Coral Gables, FL 33134 USA
info@mango.bz

For special orders, quantity sales, course adoptions and corporate sales, please email the publisher at sales@mango.bz. For trade and wholesale sales, please contact Ingram Publisher Services at customer.service@ingramcontent.com or +1.800.509.4887.

Collecting the Simpsons: The Merchandise and Legacy of Our Favorite Nuclear Family

Library of Congress Cataloging-in-Publication number: 2022937357
ISBN: (hc) 978-1-68481-053-6 (pb) 978-1-68481-320-9 (e) 978-1-68481-054-3
BISAC category code: PER004020, PERFORMING ARTS / Film / Guides & Reviews

Printed in the United States of America

Contents

Foreword

BY BILL MORRISON

In November of 1990, I was hired by 20th Century Fox Licensing and Merchandising to draw *Simpsons* characters for merchandise, to art-direct other artists, and to learn the art approvals process. I had already been taking freelance art assignments for *Simpsons* merchandise since February of that year, just a few weeks after the premiere of *The Simpsons* as a prime-time, half hour TV show. On a crisp day in February when I was given that first freelance assignment (a drawing of Bart Simpson playing the bongos, as I recall), I was told that several companies had recently taken licenses for *The Simpsons* and there was going to be a flood of merchandise released to market in the coming months, all of which would require either ready-made style guide art or custom designs and illustrations. And man, they weren't kidding! I drew a mountain of *Simpsons* art between February and November and several more mountains in the years that followed. In that first year, *The Simpsons* became a worldwide phenomenon, and *Simpsons* merch was everywhere. There was even a *Simpsons* store in Westwood, California, near the UCLA campus, that sold only *Simpsons* items.

In retrospect you would think that a salaried position with a major film studio, drawing America's newest favorite TV family would be the very definition of job security, but in 1990 that was not the case. When Fox decided they liked my stuff enough to offer me a full-time position, I remember calling my mother and telling her that I was leaving my stable studio job, where I'd been illustrating Disney movie posters, to work for Fox, where I would be drawing characters for all kinds of merchandise related to a new, hot animated show on the Fox TV network. But Mom was not impressed and cautioned me that, as popular as this new series currently was, it could be gone in a year or two, and then I'd be out of a job. She felt that Disney characters would always be popular, but *The Simpsons*? Who could tell if anyone would even remember this show in a few years? And my mom wasn't the only one who lacked confidence in *The Simpsons* back then. You can ask anyone associated with the show how long they thought it would last in those early days, and most will tell you (including creator Matt Groening himself) that they felt they'd be lucky if it lasted three seasons. There was no reason for anyone to expect the show to run more seasons than the record-holder at the time, *The Flintstones*, which aired from 1960 to 1966.

But of course, history has proven my mom and Matt Groening wrong. Thirty-three years later, *The Simpsons* is a beloved entertainment institution, a record-breaking TV legend, and still a merchandise brand of juggernaut proportions on a par with Batman and Mickey Mouse. And not to take away anything from the show itself, but I believe much of this longevity and success is owed to the merchandise and the fans who collect it. Even though the show is still popular after over three decades and still producing new episodes, I think the viewing audience has largely taken it for granted. It's sort of like an average long-lasting romance: full of heat and passion in the beginning, but warm and comfortable as time goes on. However, I still see fans getting crazy excited over the merchandise, whether it's collecting vintage items or grabbing the latest action figures, phone cases, or sneakers. That tells me that the fun and excitement of collecting the merchandise plays a big part in keeping *The Simpsons* alive and relevant.

And that's what this book is all about. *Collecting The Simpsons: The Merchandise and Legacy of Our Favorite Nuclear Family* is a celebration of an aspect of *The Simpsons* that, to this day, keeps fans energized, engaged, and passionate about the greatest animated TV show the world has ever known.

Bill Morrison

BILL JOINED THE SIMPSONS CREW IN 1990 AND INSTANTLY PLAYED A SEMINAL ROLE IN ITS GLOBAL EXPANSION AS A FRANCHISE. HE DESIGNED THE CHARACTERS FOR THE STYLE GUIDES FOR COMPANIES WHO LICENSED THE BRAND, ART-DIRECTED MERCHANDISING COMPANIES, CO-FOUNDED SIMPSONS COMICS AND DESIGNED A LARGE PERCENTAGE OF THE MERCHANDISE THAT YOU WILL SEE IN THIS BOOK.

Introduction

When *The Simpsons* debuted as bumpers on *The Tracy Ullman Show* in 1987, few could have predicted how this crudely drawn yellow family would take the world by storm. Flash forward thirty-five or so years, and *The Simpsons* is still going strong and continues to be a household name in living rooms around the world. Over that time, the Simpsons family managed to jump out of the screen and onto every commercially viable thing you could possibly imagine: comic books, video games, food, theme parks, and yes, even Pogs.

This book you hold in your hands will take you through the three-decade journey of *The Simpsons*—not as the typical "guide" you may expect, but through the history of the merchandise. You will see an exploration of the many ways the family were transformed into tangible, useful (and not so useful) goods. We will also discover that, from the very beginning, the show realized the importance (and financial upside) of having our favorite nuclear family plastered on everything from toothbrushes to ice scrapers, and why "*Simpsons* Mania" was in no way an exaggeration.

Outside of *Star Wars*, *The Simpsons* has arguably released more tie-in products than any movie or television show in history. As such, there is simply no collector on earth who can possibly claim to own every *Simpsons* toy, toothbrush, and telephone. So, while it would be impossible to include everything, we want the history and photos included within these pages to help you understand just how much stuff was and is out there. Think of it as a visual guide through the weird and wonderful world of *Simpsons* merchandise. Our hope is that it will ignite a sense of warm, fuzzy nostalgia. A nostalgia that will take you back to the days when you watched the show as a child, and the brightly colored toy aisles displaying all the things you had, all the things you wanted…and even the things you never knew existed!

About Warren

I've been collecting *Simpsons* stuff for over a decade, cataloging it online the best I can under the name Bart of Darkness (trust me, I wish there were a cool story behind the name other than it being a great episode, but there isn't). Like most kids born in the '80s, *The Simpsons* was synonymous with my childhood. The "I'm Bart Simpson, who the hell are you?" shirts, the Burger King toys, the incredible bootlegs–this stuff was impossible to miss, as if the show didn't already strike a chord with most of us. Over the years, my appreciation for the show has only expanded, as I became infatuated with the sheer volume of merchandise that the show had, and continues to produce. With that said, the majority of what you see in this book is owned by me, and lives in my personal collection. This collection and the journey surrounding it has had me put a great deal of time into really knowing and understanding the history of this section of fandom. I hope this book serves as an aid, a guide, or even just a fun distraction for each of you.

About Lydia and James

Like most of you, we grew up with *The Simpsons*. We suffered for it too, enduring Anne Robinson's *The Weakest Link* just to avoid the risk of missing *The Simpsons* at six o'clock on BBC 2 (that's if our mums hadn't got to the TV remote first!).

But if our mums succeeded, we would retreat to our bedrooms to catch up with the family in other ways: read their comics, play their video games, and even wear clothing with their faces on it.

So, when our paths crossed many years later, we had no idea of the impact the show would continue to have on our lives, even ten or so years after we were both just kids who liked *The Simpsons*.

During lockdown, in 2020 (I know, we want to forget about it too), we rewatched *The Simpsons* from start to finish. This unearthed a love for the show so strong that we decided to start a YouTube channel together called *The Simpsons Theory*. What started as a fun hobby of sharing fun videos with other like-minded fans transpired into our full-time job–and three years later, it has grown into the largest dedicated *Simpsons* channel on YouTube.

CHAPTER ONE

Toys & Beyond

WARREN EVANS

Like most hobbies, at the beginning, you don't really have a clue what kind of snowball effect you're about to unleash. Collecting for me started very small, mostly with VHS sets and the occasional flea-market Bart Simpson doll. It's incredible to think how certain things just take hold of you, and before you know it, consume a lot of your free headspace—and space in your house, for that matter. In terms of *The Simpsons*, everyone on earth has heard of it, and there is always a special connection or a bond between you and someone else who truly loves and appreciates the show on any substantial level. For me, collecting the merchandise became a way to appreciate the show beyond watching the episodes, or learning facts about the animation process. It became a window into another part of the universe and items that spoke to different eras, different interests, and different languages.

In this opening chapter, I am going to walk you through a visual guide to as many eras of merchandise as I can, starting way back in 1989. When the concept for this book first came together, we knew right away that there was no way we could cover every piece of merchandise, but rather, we could try to show you the scope of how far it reached. From my research, I would estimate that nearly 50 percent of the *Simpsons* merchandise that is still in circulation today was created and released within those first three years. The merchandising department, along with Matt Groening, pulled no punches, even in the beginning, and flooded fans with more merchandise than any parent could afford. I once interviewed longtime writer/showrunner Al Jean, and he told me that in 1990, there was a store in Los Angeles that *only* sold *Simpsons* merchandise. The moment one of you creates a working time machine, find my contact info, and let's talk.

1989

While many people immediately associate early merchandise with 1990, products do exist with the 1989 copyright. Generally speaking, these were not as exciting as what was to come, but the packaging is a great example of that special quality the show was born with. From the very beginning, it stood out from everything else on the shelf.

What I find most important about this time is that these products locked in a style and color scheme that would stick with the show for much of its early years. Without knowing exactly why, it seems to me that these simple, less premium items were possibly a quick way to get things on the toy aisle while some of the other, longer-development products were still in the making. I don't think the actual decisions made in these early stages are a point discussed often enough. Not only are the characters unique, but the fonts are rough and chunky. The colors almost hurt your eyes. Every single detail felt so different, and I think for many of us, it was hard to ignore.

© 1989 BY MATT GROENING
8·16·1989
TM & © 1989 TWENTIETH
CENTURY FOX FILM CORP.
ALL RIGHTS RESERVED.
© 1989 BEN COOPER TOYS,
A SUBSIDIARY OF
BEN COOPER, INC.
NEW YORK, NY 10010
MADE IN CHINA

DanDee (1990)

A personal favorite of mine lands right here near the beginning of our journey, and that is none other than DanDee. Founded in New Jersey in the 1950s, DanDee was mostly known for porcelain dolls and stuffed animals, as well as various seasonal items. When it comes to *The Simpsons*, however, DanDee made what I personally consider the most charming, endearing, and time-encapsulating toys and dolls the show would ever have. Everything from the sculpts to the packaging continued to build on this new and interesting brand, and for longtime collectors of the merchandise, it holds a special place.

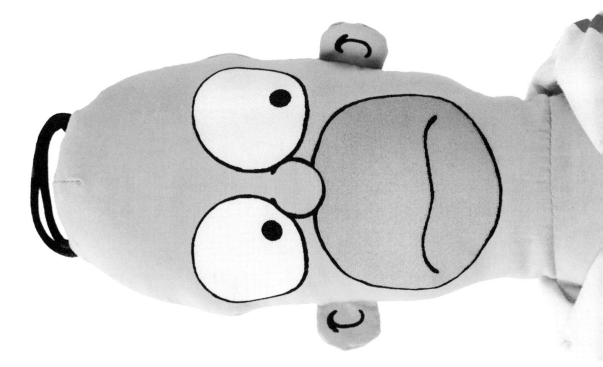

DanDee is significant for a few reasons—one being that the company was quite determined with the *Simpsons* license, and supposedly made "hundreds of samples," many of which were ultimately not released. While it may be hard to understand why these weren't released, I'm sure that in 1990, it was a lot easier to second-guess the success of merchandise for a show that barely existed. Maybe the world wasn't as eager for this volume of dolls. How could you be sure? (Again, whenever one of you completes that time machine, let's talk.) We'll talk more about this in a few chapters, so sit tight.

DanDee is also often cited as releasing the first Bart Simpson doll, the illustrious eighteen-inch Talking Bart Simpson, as well as the smaller non-talking version—one of the most easily recognized items of all show merchandise. This doll, along with a few others from that first year, stands as the main point of confusion about that lovely shade of blue used for his shirt.

One name you will hear in this book more than once is that of Bill Morrison (you might remember him from the foreword). Bill worked on art and promotional items for the merchandising department, and went on to cofound Bongo Comics with Matt Groening. He also explained one element of the blue shirt phenomenon perfectly when he told me, "Well, in the early days of the of licensing and merchandising, you had the color of Bart's shirt on the show, and a lot of the licensees would say, 'Well, this isn't going to really work with our packaging, because we've got a red background, and so we need to have some options. "

Bill also credits some of those decisions to Millie Smythe, Matt Groening's liaison during those early days. "Matt was way too busy to look at everything, but Millie would look at something, and she would have to make a decision—and if a licensee said, 'Can we put Bart in a green shirt?'—there didn't seem to be a big reason why they shouldn't or couldn't."

It's also important to note that much of this early merchandise was created, or in the process of creation, before season one had even started airing. In addition to that, the earliest Tracy Ullman short versions of Bart depicted him with a blue shirt, which mostly explains this constantly speculated-on mystery. We also see Bart wearing a green shirt in early commercials, which gets far less attention, but also exists in the merchandise.

This brings me back to how odd—in a great way—the decisions were early on. A lot of toys tried to fit into a certain market or style. You knew what they were, if they were good guys or bad guys, if they swung a sword, climbed buildings, drove a car—or maybe you could dress them up in fun outfits. But in the case of *Simpsons* merchandise, you'd have a yellow character with big eyes, odd hair, a round belly, all inside a bright green or pink box, with almost messy text. Something was very special about this combination. It matched this truly unique world that was being created for us in the show, but it also stood out so vividly in a tangible space.

When most of us look back on our childhood, I feel like it's impossible to know what made certain things jump out at us, or to remember why we begged for a specific toy. Luckily, when it comes to *The Simpsons*, I think it was something we almost didn't need to understand. The humor might have been over our heads, but that was okay. In my case, I wanted to know more instantly. There is something to that psychology, and I'm sure plenty of kids everywhere thought, "I don't know what this toy is, but my life depends on taking it home."

Mattel (1990)

In addition to DanDee, one of the most notable early lines was that of Mattel, a name synonymous with toys no matter what you collect. These also featured very bright packaging, and had commercials that I can still see in my mind: Bart sliding across the screen on top of the television, then him being stuffed in a trash can and rolled right back in the other direction by Nelson, all while the kids in the commercial create their own dialogue. Mattel is also a great example of just how hard these characters were to model out in 3D in those early days, as the smaller toys looked slightly off, in the absolute best way.

I've always had a special place in my heart for these, mostly because of the word bubble accessory. This would fit into the head of each character, which was softer than the rest of the toy, and came with multiple phrases. You could really and truly create your own scene. This also made them display even better for the adult collector, giving you something new and fresh compared to the rest of the shelf.

Mattel also made their own large dolls, but unlike DanDee, these officially included the other siblings. To me, this is also a landmark in creative packaging, with each box showing the other siblings playing with the actual toy.

I talked a bit about Bart's shirt earlier, and this set is an example of the green shirt being a thing beyond the commercials. For years, I would see discourse online about items like this being bootlegs, but you can rest assured that is untrue. The laid-back approach from the team as well as the licensees really gave us a broad palette for Bart in the beginning—and personally, I think the green is underrated!

We also talked about the green and pink packaging earlier, which would stay commonplace for several licenses over the first seven to eight years, but we saw Mattel take a different approach. The green and pink was still a major part, but against a very striking white background. I think the white packaging really shines here because it pops out extremely well against any color, especially with the bright text and full character on each card. I have to think even the most destructive kid would be tempted to hold on to the card backs, or at the very least cut out the characters for their wall.

Another mystery within the collecting community for a long time was that of the "series two" line by Mattel. It wasn't until years later that I discovered a circulated Mattel catalog promoting the line, which went on to be canceled. This line featured a much more ambitious take on the young show, with different versions of the family, including a "Baseball Bart," Homer and Marge in Hawaiian attire, and even vehicles and other characters like Krusty.

Presents by Hamilton Gifts (1990)

"Presents" by Hamilton Gifts might be the most under-appreciated line from these early days, and I have a theory as to why. Collectors a tad older than me seem to remember these being more expensive due to their market—being sold in places like Hallmark and more gift-oriented retail. The dolls came in two sizes, and as with most things, we got two versions of Bart in each size, as opposed to one like the rest of the family.

I would also go so far as to say that these are the most on model for their time, and still look fantastic today. Several years ago, the original paint masters for these dolls went up for sale, from the estate of a former employee named Rusty Lee. I was lucky enough to purchase them from a family friend, and they remain a highlight for me in the collection, but that's for another chapter.

Street Kids (1990)

Luckily for fans (and parents), some items were a tad more affordable. Street Kids is one of the companies whose products really gave you the most bang for your buck, while also being functional. If you wanted a night-light, a keychain, or even an eraser, they had something for you.

These sorts of products start to show us that the show did a lot more than just toys, even early on. This is a trend that not only speaks to this era for a lot of shows, but speaks even louder to the fun design of these characters and how hard it was to leave them in the store. When I think of my own childhood, a product based on a character like Bart that also served a practical purpose was a great way to convince your parents to buy it for you. We may have enough toys, but I sure could use a new coin bank…right?

As someone who has never worked in marketing, it seems to me that one of the smartest ideas in history was to brand non-toys with popular characters. As a former kid myself, I would enjoy brushing my teeth way more if my toothbrush had Homer on it, or actually look forward to mandatory bath time if my shampoo featured Bart's spikey hair. This would also allow the shampoo lid to double as a toy. *The Simpsons* did this as well as any property in history.

Household Products

As with functional products from companies like Street Kids, when trying to explain to someone just how far the show reached into your home, there is no better example than things for your bathroom. Everyone needs the occasional bandage, a place to keep their soap, a timer for brushing their teeth. This area of the merchandise not only aided in vital routine, but it left you with something collectible. Markets across the planet made use of this space, and with style.

This type of product became a mainstay in the merchandise for the better part of two decades. You could keep your bathroom looking nice and yellow well beyond the '90s.

Mid-Late '90s

For all the big swings the show took with the merchandise in the beginning, into the mid-'90s and beyond, there was less of a boom in the American *Simpsons* toy market, and more of a shift to different types of products. It's hard to pinpoint exactly why, but my theory is that the show began with such a large amount of merchandise, they almost needed some downtime to find the next big strategy. Or perhaps they realized its appeal beyond just kids. Regardless, this time showed a wide array of stuff, ranging from golf balls to Pogs, and included a rise in clothing and reading materials.

This is not to say that the show wasn't popular, or that there wasn't a need for new products. In my opinion, this only speaks to the growing pains of any new show. The explosion will always come at the beginning, and—much as in "Bart Gets Famous" from season five—the show had to remind fans that it was more than a "one-dimensional character with a silly catchphrase." Besides, maybe more toys would have expanded the brand less in the long term than things like comics and calendars. These types of products kept us engaged, all with another huge merchandise boom soon to follow.

COLLECTING THE SIMPSONS

International

Before we move too far out of '90s land, it is important to note that international markets for *The Simpsons* were also quite popular and an interesting space for collectors. Most countries had their hand in the *Simpsons* license, and put their own regional spin on our favorite family. International markets gave us products which feature some of the more unique packaging. Whether it was Avanti in Japan, Jemini in France, or Vivid Imaginations in England—we see new and fresh uses of the branding.

As someone who has spent the better part of a decade collecting and learning about the merchandise, something that stood out to me very early on were the many ceramic and porcelain products available across Europe in the early '90s. Lines like Harry James from the United Kingdom and Tropico from France made several of my most prized items. Whether these were coin banks, cookie jars, or butter trays, they seemingly left no stone unturned when it came to finding a way to use *The Simpsons* as a conversation piece.

If things easily broken don't speak to you, what about a product that kept you from being late to work? Wesco was a company from the UK that, among other things, specialized in clocks. A recurring theme in this chapter is the ability to make functional products beyond just toys, and everyone needs some sort of clock... especially when they don't always look like clocks!

Clocks are another fantastic representation of how much the show permeated our very existence in the '90s, because this sort of thing would be, not only great for a kid's bedroom, but a standout piece in any home, or even on your desk at work. Whether it was Homer opening a fridge, or Bart spray-painting "El Barto" on a brick wall, these clocks were dying to be on a collector's shelf, with or without batteries.

After turning off your *Simpsons* alarm clock, obviously you get up to make some coffee to start your day. While America also had plenty of *Simpsons* mugs, we see some of my favorites come from companies like Metro in Australia and Tropico in France. Who wouldn't feel extra in-tune with that first cup of coffee with designs like this?

While some of the American mugs felt truer to form, I always loved the slight variation of color and decision-making when it came to mugs like this. It's almost as if they were working with a completely different color palette at times. If there is one thing you grow to appreciate with this hobby, it is the way each market seemingly had its own tendencies. Just look at how wonderfully muted those Metro colors are!

The influence from these types of international products wasn't lost on America, as we see things like cookie jars come around in the late '90s, including two of my favorite products:

Once again, we see the show go well beyond function and back again. Outside of your home, you could find the Simpsons on plenty of snacks. In this case, it wouldn't be much of an international product discussion if I didn't feature the notorious C.C. Lemon lunchbox.

For some time, there was confusion about the origin of this lunchbox, mostly because C.C. Lemon isn't widely available outside of Japan. Many collectors, like myself, originally assumed it was a company known for things like this, when in reality it is a very well-branded beverage company! As far as the lunchbox goes, this wasn't even a product you could initially purchase, but something you could win via giveaway. This tin lunchbox also stands out because of the 3D heads coming off of the 2D family on the couch, which is unlike most products in this space. In the years since, they have become easier to find, but remain one of my favorite uses of the family.

World of Springfield (2000)

As we come out of the '90s, we enter into what some fans and collectors consider the best toy line ever made—none other than World of Springfield by Playmates. Playmates was no stranger to successful toys, making stuff for properties like *Teenage Mutant Ninja Turtles*, *Darkwing Duck*, and *Star Trek*. They gave *The Simpsons* the same treatment, and in a line that perfectly spanned the universe of Springfield and really connected fans more than ever to each individual character.

Playmates not only made action figures, but much as with TMNT, they paid a lot of attention to things that enhanced the experience. For the first time, we had a toy line that could not only interact with environments, but actually speak! Each series came with playsets which, when connected to, could deliver lines from each character. The first series featured the whole family, plus Krusty, Mr. Burns, and an additional version of Homer.

This first line had Homer saying iconic lines like, "Boy, everyone is stupid except me," and, "Weaseling out of things is important to learn." The line also had Mr. Burns saying, "I prefer the hands-on touch you only get with hired goons," and Krusty saying, "So, I'll just make some more money; crank out some cheesy merchandise." Oh, and obviously Bart says, "Aye caramba!" and "Cool your jets, man!" among other things.

One of the many cool features of the WOS line is that, not only did everyone speak, but they said different things depending on what environment they were connected to. This made it really hard for these to ever get boring, and I also believe it is one of the reasons the line is still so collectible. Between 207 figures, you could hear 1,042 different phrases!

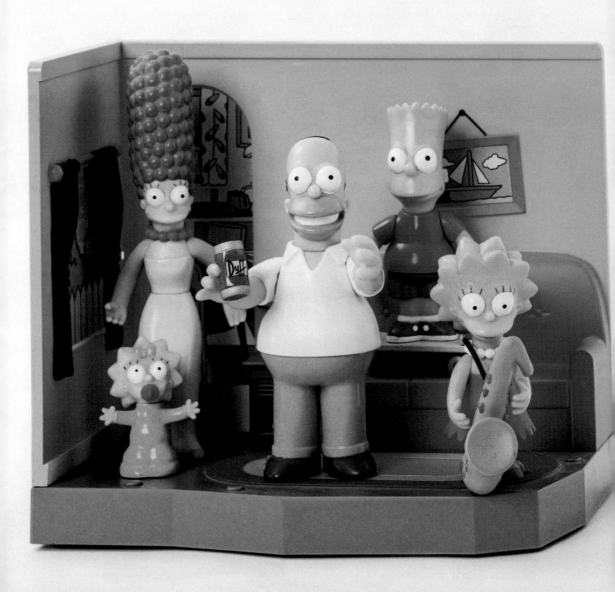

Playmates also pulled out references to our favorite episodes like never before, giving us sets to complete via mail-away in addition to the sets you could get in store. A personal favorite of mine is the Be Sharps set.

Figures like this remind us how deep the *Simpsons* world can go, and how many episodes are burned into our minds in their entirety. I mean, who doesn't want to hear Barney say, "Barbershop is in danger of growing stale. I'm taking it to strange new places," or Skinner saying, "Only one question remains, gentlemen; what do we call ourselves?"

This is also where we see even more of a growing interest in things specific to Treehouse of Horror, and Playmates made *several* sets featuring these obscure characters. This line also allowed us to own actual toys featured in the show for the first time, like this Talking Krusty doll—complete with good/evil switch!

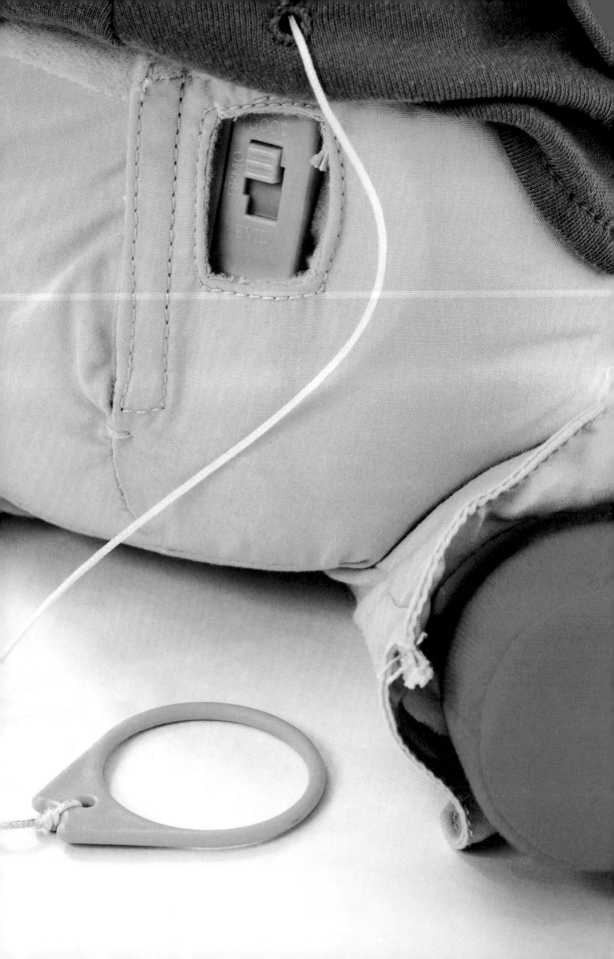

This is an area I wish they had focused on even more within the show. It seems like there could have been plenty of money in a licensed sailboat painting, or corn cob curtains! Just think about a big cutout of Bart showcasing his "Krusty the Clown Collection," complete with sheet set, poster, wall clock, and so much more. These are the ideas that keep me up at night.

All in all, Playmates gave us a line with over 250 pieces, and found no character or reference too obscure for a figure. To my mind, it is one of the most interesting runs of any property or toy company, because it saw a need for more than toys of just Homer, Marge, Bart, Lisa, and Maggie—it showed that fans also cared about a Captain McCallister figure, or even a Super Nintendo—I mean Superintendent Chalmers figure. These steps only opened up possibilities for all who made stuff after, or even during, their run.

It is still unclear exactly why Playmates decided to end its *Simpsons* run. Many attribute it to things like "collectors' fatigue"—this is more or less where the sheer volume of a line becomes overwhelming, as does the need for space to display it. Others believe it was because the line reached further and further into the depths of Springfield for new pieces, leaving characters like Database in later series to pile up on the shelves.

As someone who truly loves this hobby and line, I wish we had only known what we were missing out on. The following sets and figures are just a few things that were set to be released, had the line continued:

- Rabbi Krustofski

- Lyle Lanley

- Stonecutter Wiggum

- Stonecutter Hall with Stonecutter Carl

- Series seventeen with Ninja Bart, Richard, Lewis, Arnie Pie, Bigfoot Homer, Flying Hellfish Grandpa, and Cecil Terwilliger

- School Playground with Janey

- Oval Office based on "Bart To The Future" with President Lisa, Old Homer and Marge, Adult Bart, and Maggie Jr.

- Treehouse of Horror featuring the "House of Pain" with Walrus Homer, Eagle Lisa, Spider Bart, Anteater Maggie, and Panther Marge

- Series eighteen with Lindsey Naegle, Tuxedo Kang, Tuxedo Kodos, Uncle Moe, Sanjay, and Akira

- Flanders Rumpus Room with Maude Flanders

COLLECTING THE SIMPSONS

SERIES # 16

THE SIMPSONS ™

WORLD OF SPRINGFIELD INTERACTIVE FIGURE

Ages 4 and up
Asst. No. 99480

Playmates

*INTELLI-TRONIC
VOICE ACTIVATION

Stock No. 99484

I'm a big fat dynamo.

EVIL HOMER

PLACE EVIL HOMER ON ANY COMPATIBLE
WORLD OF SPRINGFIELD ENVIRONMENT
TO HEAR HIM TALK.*

"Figures "talk" only when connected to compatible environments – (sold separately).

During and beyond Playmates, we saw another rise in collectibles for adults. Companies like Hamilton also dug deep into reference land for a totally different type of merchandise. These sculptures were often limited and hand-numbered on the bottom, making them something for the shelf, or even the glass case. These feel unique even among the more fragile products, certainly due to the lower production runs and smaller frequency of finding certain pieces.

Hamilton also branched out into sub-set lines like "Couch Gags"—some of the rarest and most beloved pieces of this era. This took a fan-favorite staple of episodes and gave you a way to look at them in 3D. My only complaint is that they didn't make them all!

Hamilton Collection (2001)

Whether it was Homer watching the game, or the family in the style of *The Wizard of Oz*, Hamilton paid absurd attention to detail, down to the can tab or the potato chip bag. They were also quite easy to break. Probably best to keep your kids as far away from these as possible, because sadly, with great detail comes... great responsibility?

McFarlane Toys (2006)

Much like what Playmates did with World of Springfield, as we moved into the later 2000s, we saw companies like McFarlane Toys step into this space. McFarlane, which had a reputation for making very poseable, detailed toys in more of a superhero space, brought a new take to *Simpsons* merchandise. This included things like a magnetic, customizable couch gag, as well as the well-loved Ironic Punishment set that allowed Homer to actually eat the donuts!

With this reference to a fan favorite, you could turn a crank and watch the donuts fall into Homer's mouth (although sometimes they might miss, classic Homer)—the donuts would then fall into a compartment in his stomach that you could empty when you were done and then set them up again. Quite a lot of work, but worth it to make yourself laugh…and your friends! Obviously your friends…

Kid Robot (2008)

In addition to McFarlane, we also saw Kidrobot come onto the scene. Kidrobot stands out to most because, unlike other lines in this chapter, they mostly worked in a blind-box space. This means that every box you buy has a bit of mystery, and you may or may not get the one you want. Not everyone appreciates or enjoys this model, but I've always thought it added to the fun. It raised the stakes and allowed you to trade with friends to fill out your collection. The first wave of their *Simpsons* line was released in 2008, and they put out products for well over a decade.

In addition to a second wave featuring even more of Springfield, Kidrobot also tapped into the love for Treehouse of Horror, with an entire wave featuring Kang and Kodos, Panther Marge, Zombie Krusty, Bart the Fly, and so many more, once again requiring a bit of luck to complete the set. They also went on to do a twenty-fifth anniversary line, as well as an entire line set around Moe's Tavern. Despite the uncertainty, these are loved by many, and I can almost hear your keyboard clicking away as you begin your search.

If you are one of those who don't enjoy the uncertainty of a blind box, Kidrobot also released larger versions of some of the more popular toys. Unlike with the smaller figures, you knew exactly what you were getting. You were also getting it at about ten times the size, and who doesn't love that?

Beyond that, in recent years, Kidrobot has made what I consider two shining stars in this entire hobby: Stupid Sexy Flanders, in two colorways—a traditional, true-to-the-episode palette, as we well as a bright neon pink/yellow combination—and a very specific Itchy & Scratchy toy for the "My Bloody Valentine" short, which is easily one of my favorite items in this book.

COLLECTIBLE VINYL FIGURE

Super7 (2021)

Luckily for all of us, *Simpsons* toys are alive and well—especially thanks to companies like Super7, which has taken a familiar yet enhanced approach to the license. With two different styles of figures, there is something for every type of collector. If you want to get that reference just right, the Ultimates line makes that possible, each figure coming with multiple heads, hands, and accessories.

In the natural evolution of *Simpsons* products, it makes sense that these would be on another level. With its extreme attention to detail—which is another theme throughout several of these lines, but in a completely new way—clearly made by fans and for fans, this one feels almost personal. I like that.

Super7 is also known for its ReAction line of figures, made in a classic 3.75" scale that would make a collector of any age nostalgic. Each set has a theme, and with that the card art changes, making no two sets the same. This is something we rarely saw in earlier lines, and makes an excellent point about how much collecting has progressed. More than just creators being fans, we see collectors becoming the people making things for other collectors, and it really shows.

I find this sort of thing extremely important, because this progression only means a higher quality, and value that isn't fleeting. Obviously, value shouldn't be the driving force for collecting, but it adds a layer of insurance to a hobby that isn't always cheap. This is exactly why it's important to create a product that brings joy, but that is also held to a high standard. We see all sides of that triangle over the more than thirty years of merchandise, and things only continue to look up.

Closing Thoughts

So there you have it! Now you can talk about this stuff with your friends, impress them with your newfound knowledge, or even just add a few new items to your want-list. Oh wait…this is only the first chapter. We still have so much ground to cover. Now that we've talked about the toys, let's take an even deeper look.

CHAPTER TWO

Clothing & Fashion

LYDIA HICKS

Being a kid in the early '90s, there weren't many TV characters you could really relate to, or *wanted* to relate to. The high-schoolers in *Scooby-Doo* felt outdated, the babies in *The Rugrats* were…well, babies. And without them, we were left with some Teenage Mutant Ninja Turtles and an abundance of other cartoon animals and superheroes. That's not to say we loved them any less, but we might not have felt quite as cool wearing their faces on a T-shirt—especially during those formative years where the goal was to identify yourself and, let's face it, feel "cool."

So when *The Simpsons* arrived with striking aesthetics, contemporary humor, adult themes and relatable characters, kids finally had a "cool" cartoon to like, and a character to idolize: Bart Simpson.

This is partly why I feel "Bartmania" hit young people specifically, and why the general success of *The Simpsons* in fashion centers around Bart. There was no other character who had confidence, heart, and daring humor balanced with the dark flaws that come with being a child. In short, wearing a T-shirt with Bart's face on your chest felt even more empowering than the likes of Superman.

The full power of Bartmania was unleashed when *The Simpsons* merchandise hit the shelves, which of course included Bart Simpson T-shirts. But amongst them was one displaying Bart's proud confession of being an "underachiever, man." Kids loved it. For them, wearing such a statement felt like a prepubescent and political act of self-expression… Which is exactly why adults hated it. And so, Bart was put into detention in real life when schools across the USA banned Bart Simpson T-shirts.

"FRIENDS SPOTTED IT THE MOMENT I STEPPED OFF THE BUS, MOUTHS AGAPE IN TOTAL DISBELIEF THAT MY PARENTS HAD EVER APPROVED THE PURCHASE. I DIDN'T GET IT, ESPECIALLY SINCE IT SEEMED LIKE HALF THE SCHOOL WAS DONNING SIMILAR BART SIMPSON GEAR. BUT WITHIN THE WEEK, I COULDN'T WEAR THAT SHIRT TO SCHOOL ANYMORE. BART SIMPSON HAD BEEN BANNED, AND LITTLE DID I KNOW, MY SMALL MIDWESTERN TOWN WAS CAUGHT IN A NATIONWIDE WAVE OF KNEE-JERK RESPONSE TO PREPUBESCENT SELF-EXPRESSION."

—MARK WILSON FOR FAST COMPANY MAGAZINE

THESE ORIGINAL BANNED T-SHIRTS FROM 1989 HAVE ONLY CATAPULTED IN VALUE, AND YOU COULD BE LOOKING TO SPEND UPWARDS OF $150!

The Banned Bart Simpson T-Shirt

Principal William Krumnow was in his office at Lutz Elementary School in Ohio, his finger poised over the school intercom button. It was April 1990, late into the school year, and the children sat at their desks oblivious to the dread that adults felt everywhere. Who knew that the new kid on the block, the one with buggy eyes and yellow skin, trapped inside the TV set, would put so much pressure on the principal? It seemed that life was now replicating art, as Krumnow now felt a bit like Principal Seymour Skinner.

And so, with his voice embiggened over the school intercom, Principal Krumnow announced that Bart Simpson T-shirts were now banned.

The specific T-shirt that caused the uproar showed the little hooligan aiming a slingshot at anyone who dared stare with the words "underachiever, and proud of it, man".

To the principal, this was an unnecessary rebellion in a place of learning. "To be proud of being an incompetent is a contraction of what we stand for," Krumnow told *Deseret News*. "We strive for excellence and to instill good values in kids… The show teaches the wrong things to students."

This shared response terminated other Bart Simpson T-shirts with slogans such as "Eat My Shorts," "I didn't do it. Nobody saw me do it. You can't prove anything!" and "I'm Bart Simpson. Who the hell are you?" along with any other clothes that bared the little guy's face.

Many schools in Florida, California, Michigan, Illinois, and Washington, DC, followed suit in declaring their own war on Bart Simpson. Their hope was to save children from being tainted by America's breakout bad boy who was, by all of *their* accounts, the worst kind of role model for kids to emulate.

UCLA professor Gordon Berry was interviewed at the time, and said, "If I had my option, the T-shirt would say: 'I'm Bart Simpson. I'm an underachiever and I'm trying to do better.' But that's not much fun, is it?"

All of a sudden, the Helen Lovejoys of society were having a moment of mourning for the sanctity of America's children.

"WON'T SOMEONE PLEASE THINK OF THE CHILDREN?" —HELEN LOVEJOY

But perhaps the question should have been, "What did the *children* think?" And with that Chris Bury, from ABC News, took to the schools. "It's just a cartoon, we won't act like Bart Simpson," one smart child earnestly told Bury (most likely with a slingshot hidden under his hat). But for every Bart champion, you had a Martin Prince, "If you're an underachiever, you shouldn't be proud of it."

Psychologist, Dr. Barbara Kadow, provided a counterargument against her fellow adults: "This is something that children can grab onto and identify with… If Bart's having problems and making it and doing okay, maybe I can make it and do alright, too," supporting the argument that, even if Bart Simpson is not the brightest, best-behaved student, he can still thrive in a pretty terrifying world, and be proud of who he is.

A gift from Bart Simpson himself (a.k.a., Nancy Cartwright) to Warren after completing the interview for *Simpsons Is Greater Than…* "To say I was excited, nervous, and in slight disbelief, would be an understatement. And over the course of the interview, we discovered that we wore the exact same hat size: 7⅝… A few weeks later, she sent me this hat."

The Simpsons React

Amidst the hysteria, FOX TV issued their own statement addressing the schools' T-shirt ban, "FOX TV will say only that Bart respects elementary school principals—even the ones who have nothing better to do than tell kids what to wear."

Little did FOX know that sticking up for the Simpsons family against angry adults would become a regular occurrence. In fact, in the same year, "Marge Simpson" had to defend her family against former First Lady Barbara Bush in the form of a letter. But it still didn't stop President Bush famously declaring that American families should be "closer to the Waltons than the Simpsons" just two years later in 1992.

The Simpsons was a break-out prime-time television show, and its exposure was bound to reach those who just were *never* going to enjoy it. Especially if those audiences had grown up with the more traditional, conservative family values of *The Waltons*. Naturally, seeing Bart mooning his principal or an openly alcoholic father shocked the airwaves… even though these characters were a far more accurate portrayal of us than the squeaky-clean Walton family would ever be.

Nancy Cartwright, the voice of Bart Simpson, spoke on *The Simpsons Is Greater Than…* podcast about confronting worried mothers at a football game amidst the controversy. They were worried about their children watching *The Simpsons*. But she explained that, as a mother she empathized with them, but also emphasised that it is the parents' job to teach them right from wrong, not a TV show.

Later on, in 2014, Matt Groening discussed the T-shirt ban in an interview with *Entertainment Weekly*. Interestingly, he was joined by *Family Guy*'s Seth Macfarlane in a discussion on the outrage surrounding *The Simpsons*' back in the '90s—compared to *Family Guy*'s humor today: "We got in trouble for Bart wearing an 'Underachiever and Proud of It, Man' T-shirt. That's because cartoons up until *The Simpsons* had been aimed at children. One of the smartest things that we did was insist that it's for adults, with the idea that there are a lot of smart kids out there who will get jokes that grown-ups get."

So maybe the kids who liked *The Simpsons* were not "underachievers" after all, but incredibly smart—we will take that one, Mr. Groening.

Was Bart Really a Threat?
A '90s Kid Retrospective

To me, Bart was just an entertaining, funny, and cool kid. But I could also see that, even if he did get into trouble, he pretty much always did the right thing in the end. We only have to look at episodes such as season two's "Bart Gets An F" or season seven's "Marge Be Not Proud" where the focus is on Bart having to find his way to the right path, whether it be studying for a test or getting his mother a truly thoughtful Christmas present.

This is why it baffles me that so many parents were worried about *The Simpsons*. It was perhaps the only cartoon that we could all really relate to, including our parents. It was a show full of human experiences, and to see characters just like us make mistakes, but then face the consequences, always had such a big impact on me. I don't necessarily remember how or why Bart got into trouble, but I certainly remember the disappointment on Marge's face or how real it felt for Bart to still fail a test he had tried so hard to pass.

It has been over three decades since the T-shirt ban, and Bart Simpson has arguably become the Elvis of our era. This was a little guy who caused mischief around the world without leaving the TV screen, and he didn't even have to wiggle his hips to "Hound Dog."

A Bart Simpson T-shirt represents a safe but powerful mischievousness; a harmless rebellion that probably feels more relevant to emulate now than it did back then. For now we have crappy jobs, governments, and bosses that I'm sure we would be more than happy to moon at, or ask to eat our shorts. This is perhaps why, in thrift shops across the globe, if you were to find an original 1989 banned Bart T-shirt, you could expect to pay upwards of $150. Oh, the price of a slice of harmless, nostalgic rebellion.

Bootleg Bart—The Phenomenon

There is no question that a lot of money can be made with *Simpsons* merchandise. But in the '90s specifically, products were flying off the shelves quicker than stores could stock them. This intense demand branched out and created a black-market of entrepreneurs who all wanted a piece of the pie. Soon there were unlicensed t-shirts, figurines, books, plushies, and so much more. Who would have known that, like Homer as Pie Man, bootleggers everywhere would give the *Simpsons* brand its own pie in the face in the form of warped, strange, but undeniably interesting designs?

This specific merchandise was a phenomenon in its own right. When a show has such an influence on popular imagery, anything is possible, and that is exactly the mantra bootleg T-shirt designers adopted. You had the artists who simply replicated the designs from the show, but with some accidental (and sometimes hilarious) irregularities; or you had those who would plant the characters in situations ten times wackier than the episodes. Weird, trashy, or political situations. All of a sudden Bart (or "Rambart") was defeating the Iraqi army single-handedly, exclaiming "Kiss my crack, Iraq!"; drawn Black with his hair in dreadlocks and renamed "Bart Marley"; and was even engulfed by a large lady's butt.

The focus on Bart links back to the world's obsession of him and the aforementioned 'Bartmania'. The way that the world's most rambunctious boy was being made even more scandalous, on such a large scale, showed that designers saw a potential in Bart that no other mainstream TV character had had before. He was an icon for pushing boundaries, and whose personality seemed to lend itself to such political statements.

Never before had artists taken real ownership of a mainstream character and warped him into their own edgy ideals; it's no wonder these original designs are marveled at by the heads of streetwear fashion brands: "Bootleg counterfeit shirts featuring everyone's favorite '90s TV family *The Simpsons* are a piece of American history. Period. There is more to it than just an off-looking graphic printed on a cheap T-shirt… It's a piece of pop culture. Just like the show itself," said Caiza Andresen, Brand Consultant for OBEY, writing for *Title Mag*.

"Black Bart" in Bootleg Merchandise

The boundless selling potential of Bart Simpson T-shirts, and the number of people wanting to capitalize on it, led to some truly rogue and controversial designs—one subgenre in particular being "Black Bart."

The designers typically drew Black Bart wearing gold chains, kufi hats, Africa-shaped necklaces, and with a high-top fade. He was also shown high-fiving Nelson Mandela, quoting Public Enemy, and playing for the Chicago Bulls. This trend in designs highlighted that Bart Simpson was quickly celebrated by the Black community. Matt Groening himself supported the embrace, saying, "Bart is like Santa Claus. No one really knows what color he is."

In 1990, *The New York Times* published an article theorizing why this movement was happening. Russell Adams, the chairman of the Afro-American Studies department at Howard University, said that Bart was, above all, an anti-establishment figure: "There is a suppressed rage in the cartoon that Black people are picking up on."

Ernest White, a talk show host for WDCU-FM, Washington, DC, added, "I guess this presence of the Black Bart T-shirt says there is an association with the underdog, a need to fight the establishment."

However, a 1991 academic paper by Peter Parisi entitled " 'Black Bart' Simpson: Appropriation and Revitalization in Commodity Culture" suggested that the Black Bart imagery was "the most popular Afrocentric appropriation of mass culture iconography" and that little merchandise appeared to be created by Black people themselves. Moreover, with the popularity of Black Bart, even the bootlegs were bootlegged, and variations were created out of commercial self-interest rather than authentic participation.

Untangling the layers upon layers of appropriation and reappropriation heaped upon each other more than thirty years later is arduous. Some could view Black Bart as artful mischief, cheap entrepreneurial opportunism, or an inhibiting force against innovation…or it could simply fall under all three.

Bootlegging Now

"Bootleg Bart" T-shirts all have something in common. Even though their production may have started as a simple, opportunistic way to earn money, they are all commentary in cotton tee form. The artists' concentration on Bart's signature traits—his dislike for authority and "the man," as well as his general mischief—aligns itself with the wearer in a way that no other character could represent. In fact, the point of Bootleg Bart is not an attempt to trick people into buying a fake Bart shirt, but to offer a fake Bart shirt that is incontestably fake and obviously cooler than the legally sanctioned options made by huge corporations. And what is more Bart Simpson than that?

As technology progressed, it became far easier to source such T-shirts online, not only for vintage '90s bootlegs (which are sometimes more valuable than the licensed merchandise) but also fresh and sophisticated designs from creators today. If you dig deep enough into the corners of the *Simpsons* community on social media, you can find bootleggers who pride themselves on designing clothing with more subtle references to the show. Such T-shirt designs include retro-style tour merchandise for Hullabalooza, ads for Springfield's Monorail, Canyonero, and even staff T-shirts for Hank Scorpio's Globex Corporation.

Bootleg Bart's Biggest Fan: Matt Groening

You might be surprised to learn that Matt Groening—yes, *the* creator of *The Simpsons*—loves a bit of Bootleg Bart. "Let me be careful here. I like it. I'm not endorsing it. I find it hilarious," Groening said for *Entertainment Weekly*.

Why? Well, Groening has said the "badness of it makes me laugh," which is a reason why many hold these otherwise misunderstood relics of art in such high acclaim. In fact, he even has his own collection, and has spoken about one particular favorite piece of his own bootleg merchandise: "I've got this Bart Simpson figurine of Bart—I think it's an Easter theme—Bart is sitting on a bunch of eggs, but they've painted him not the *Simpsons* yellow, but a pink Caucasian color, and the eggs are also pink. So it looks like he has multiple testicles."

The Simpsons Crew and Celebrity Guest-Star Varsity Jacket

Imagine being in *The Simpsons*. You will be immortalized in the world's most beloved TV show, have eternal bragging rights, have your own character design, and be in the possession of the coveted *Simpsons* Guest-Star Varsity Jacket.

These varsity jackets or "crew jackets" were exclusively produced for cast and crew and never got released or sold publicly. They have 100 percent genuine leather sleeves, a 100 percent wool body, and a 100 percent cool rating with the whole family embroidered proudly on the back.

When the show was first released, the studio sent out these jackets with just one special character patch. They then sent a new patch annually with each season, so depending on the season you joined, you would have that many patches already attached to the jacket. When it came to the arrival of your new patch, it would be joined by a letter from the studio with instructions as to where to place it. We are lucky to be in contact with staff who showed us their letter when receiving Seymour and Agnes Skinner:

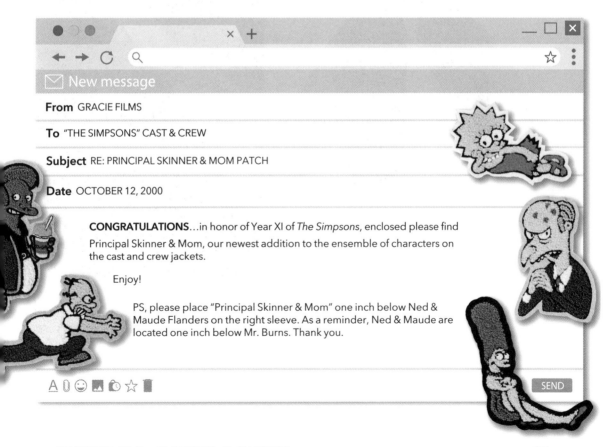

From GRACIE FILMS

To "THE SIMPSONS" CAST & CREW

Subject RE: PRINCIPAL SKINNER & MOM PATCH

Date OCTOBER 12, 2000

CONGRATULATIONS…in honor of Year XI of *The Simpsons*, enclosed please find Principal Skinner & Mom, our newest addition to the ensemble of characters on the cast and crew jackets.

Enjoy!

PS, please place "Principal Skinner & Mom" one inch below Ned & Maude Flanders on the right sleeve. As a reminder, Ned & Maude are located one inch below Mr. Burns. Thank you.

So if you worked on or starred in the show up until around 2005, when they were sadly discontinued, you would have been sent one with the full fifteen attachable character patches already attached.

The patches we've seen on various jackets, worn by guest-stars such as Susan Sarandon and Woody Harrelson, include Homer Simpson, Marge Simpson, Milhouse, Edna Krabappel, Bart Simpson, Apu Nahasapeemapetilon, Troy McClure, Lisa Simpson, Montgomery Burns, Ned Flanders, Maude Flanders, and Seymour and Agnes Skinner.

Unfortunately, these varsity jackets aren't produced anymore. But if you have enough luck, drive, or dough, you could get yourself an existing one secondhand. The latest one I've found dates back to 2004, owned by Jerry Lewis for his performance in season fifteen's "Treehouse of Horror XIV," which sold for $768 at an estate auction. But the most expensive one I found belonged to Steve Martin, given to him in 1998 for his performance in the 200th episode, "Trash of the Titans," which was sold for $2,560.

Here is Warren's jacket, which he found a few years ago. The embroidered name "Al" stands for Al Ovadia, the former merchandising president for The Simpsons and FOX. It also turned out that this was one of the original seventy-five jackets made, and given out as Christmas presents by none other than Matt Groening.

THE SIMPSONS

100

EPISODES

Another crew jacket given exclusively to staff in 1992 commemorating the 100th episode, "Sweet Seymour Skinner's Badasssss Song" (Season 7, Episode 19).

How *The Simpsons* Inspired Streetwear

Let's face it. *The Simpsons* is just cool. It is a striking cartoon, not just in terms of its heart, humor, and storytelling, but also its look. There are distinct color palettes, graphic design choices, and fonts which capture the style and nostalgia of the '90s. As the show has progressed, these elements have been made cleaner to suit the evolution of animation technology, but there is still something very special about its aesthetics. So much so, that *The Simpsons* not only caught our attention, flicking through the channels, but also streetwear designers all over the world.

The term "streetwear" was first used in the 1990s to describe a style of clothing inspired by the hip-hop and skate cultures of New York City as well as Californian surf culture. Its focus on graphics and logos appealed to the youth eager to express themselves, combined with the benefit of casual comfort to skate or surf. And with *The Simpsons*'s existing clean and vibrant graphics, along with its carefree and cool protagonist, Bart Simpson (who famously skateboarded), it's no wonder why the streetwear movement soon adopted *The Simpsons* in its rise to popularity.

Before Bart, there was no other TV character that really represented those who wanted to break the mold of society and challenge authority while still being lighthearted and fun. So when we saw skater-style five-panel snapbacks for sale with our new favorite character, we knew we wouldn't be able to show we were cool without Bart stuck right on top of our heads.

Sneaker culture was also a rising icon in streetwear, so Bart Simpson was soon branded on us literally head-to-toe. Dunlop came out with their first *Simpsons* high-top trainers in 1991.

Simpsons trainers only became more popular, with more and more brands using the *Simpsons* IP to innovate their designs with its unique aesthetics. These included sneaker fashion giants Nike, Adidas, Vans, and Converse all releasing their own lines with multiple *Simpsons* line releases.

People didn't want *Simpsons* clothing simply to show their love of the show, but because they loved the designs and the graphics it inspires. This made consumers and designers take the show more seriously than any other media personality—even Mickey Mouse! Brands like BAPE, Levi's, Supreme, and UNIQLO have all released numerous clothing collections featuring *Simpsons* characters and graphics.

The Simpsons's impact on fashion has also been seen in high fashion, with designers such as Jeremy Scott, who incorporated the show for his Moschino collection in 2012. Scott, known for his colorful and conceptual designs with nods to pop culture, looked to Bart Simpson and 1990s technology for his fall 2012 collection.

In interviews, Scott talked about how the kids who wore the Bart Simpson T-shirts back in the '90s were still "the cool kids." He also spoke about how fashion always comes back around, reaffirming the point that Bartmania extends past the show and the episodes; it was a movement that inspired all ages and genders. Which is why even we adults wouldn't be put off wearing a shirt with a character on it that we loved as kids.

Closing Thoughts

The Simpsons brand knows no bounds in merchandising, we know that; this entire book proves it. But wearing clothing with the Simpsons on it suggests a subconscious or conscious effort to allow the show to help shape your identity and insert it into your day-to-day life. Whether you're a nine-year-old wanting to emulate the confidence of Bart, a thirty-something who loves the faded prints and colors from a simpler time, a forty-year-old parent wearing Homer Simpson slippers that were a gift from the kids, or simply someone who wishes to insert some much-needed Simpsons humor into your mundane life and wardrobe.

Whatever the reason may be, you know that no matter the age, if you see someone wearing a *Simpsons* T-shirt, chances are that you could shout a random quote, and be met with the following line: "Dental Plan!"– "Lisa Needs Braces," and so forth. At the end of the day, us weirdos need to communicate somehow.

Bart The General
Moaning Lisa

The Crepes Of Wrath
Krusty Gets Busted

The Best Of
THE SIMPSONS
Volumes 1, 2, and 3

FOX VIDEO

The Best Of
THE SIMPSONS™
Volumes 4, 5 and 6

Tree House of Horror
(The Simpsons Halloween Special)
Bart Gets an F

Two Cars in Every Garage and
Three Eyes on Every Fish
Bart Vs. Thanksgiving

Bart the Daredevil
Itchy, Scratchy & Marge

20 CENTURY FOX
HOME ENTERTAINMENT™

THE SIMPSONS
Volumes 7, 8 and 9

Bart Gets Hit by a Car
One Fish, Two Fish, Blowfish,
Blue Fish

The Way We Was
Homer Vs. Lisa and the 8th
Commandment

Three Men and a Comic Book
Lisa's Substitute

Catalog #4104450   20 CENTURY FOX
HOME ENTERTAINMENT™

...ONS
... and 12

...ashington
... Failed

...lerer
... e Clown

...rror II
...

THE SIMPSONS

Halloween
Treehouse of Horror III
Treehouse of Horror V

Springfield Murder Mysteries
Black Widower
Cape Feare

Heaven & Hell
Bart Sells His Soul
Lisa The Skeptic

TRICK OR TREEHOUSE

THE SIMPSONS
POLITICAL PARTY

Volume I
Sideshow Bob Roberts
Trash of the Titans

Volume II
Two Bad Neighbors
Duffless

Volume III
I Love Lisa
The Trouble With Trillions

20 CENTURY FOX
HOME ENTERTAINMENT

S...
GO HO...

Marg...
A Stre...

Whe...

B...
Kru...

CHAPTER THREE

Home Media

JAMES HICKS

Like any kid in the '90s armed with a VHS cassette and tape player, I would, on the *odd* occasion, record a *Simpsons* episode off the television. (The statute of limitations has passed by now, right?)

With the invention of VHS, home media viewership changed forever. These little black boxes were compact, easy to use, and (most importantly) affordable. Families were able to create their own personal video libraries, and for me, collecting episodes of *The Simpsons* became my obsessive hobby. Whenever an episode was about to air, I would insert any tape I had to hand (whether it had "Wedding" or "Baby's First Steps" written on it or not) and record it.

Alas, without easy internet access, or even the "info" feature on TV, I never knew what the official episode was called, instead scribbling the vague plot on the VHS label, i.e., "Sideshow Bob Episode #4" or "Dental Plan… Lisa needs braces." I know it wasn't ideal, but I was still satisfied with my catch of the day, and embarked on another search for a VHS tape to overwrite. (Sorry, Mum!)

But for the more noble among us, who struggled with this ethical dilemma—much like Lisa's conscience in season two's "Homer vs. Lisa and the 8th Commandment"—you could buy official releases from FOX themselves.

It's undeniable that watching these official FOX VHS releases was far more enjoyable. The tapes could sustain being played red-raw, the covers were designed with new illustrations of the family, and you knew exactly what episodes were on the tape… without the risk of your aunt's wedding vows interrupting right when Mr. Burns's shooter was about to be revealed.

VHS—Be Kind, Rewind

Did you know that the first VHS set of *The Simpsons* was released, not in the USA, but Europe? Released on October 1, 1991, "The *Simpsons* Collection" was a volume of fourteen VHS tapes featuring episodes from seasons one, two, and three.

It wasn't until 1997 that FOX released "The Best of *The Simpsons*" for Region 1 USA, and this was a one-to-twelve-volume set that concluded in 1999. Due to the limitations of the technology, they could only fit a couple of episodes onto one tape, so they came in a cardboard box that fitted three tapes.

It is mind-boggling to consider that only two decades later, your small cell phone, that fits neatly inside your pants pocket, can access over seven hundred episodes through the Disney+ app.

But the great thing about these tapes is that they sometimes also featured Tracy Ullman shorts as bumpers, as well as commercials for other *Simpsons* products. FOX also released a series of *Simpsons* VHSs that contained a collection of themed episodes. "Springfield Murder Mysteries," released in 1999, contained a collection of episodes like, "Who Shot Mr. Burns?" and "Cape Feare." Another notable example is "Bart Wars—The Simpsons Strike Back" which focused on episodes that have *Star Wars* references.

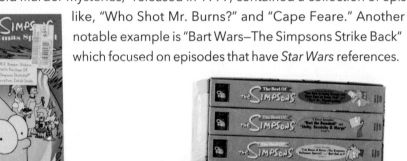

But alas, VHS didn't live forever. A better, newer technology hit the shelves, knocking poor VHS off its perch and into the bargain bin: DVDs. DVDs were more compact, had clearer picture quality and better storage, and best yet, didn't require rewinding.

DVDs really overtook VHS tapes in sales in 2002, and once DVD players became more affordable, there was really no reason to ever watch a VHS tape again. And so VHS was relegated to boxes in closets everywhere.

DVDs

When the first season of *The Simpsons* was released on DVD in 2001, it quickly became the bestselling TV DVD set in history. It not only featured all the episodes in the first season, but also had the benefit of tons of behind-the-scenes goodness. These included storyboards, commercials, and deleted scenes, showing us never-seen-before glimpses into the making of our favorite show. But one of the biggest features was episode commentary from *Simpsons* staff and voice actors. They were essentially podcasts before podcasts were a thing, and made us fans feel closer to the show we adored.

Each DVD box set that followed was massively popular too. We could go back and revisit the show whenever we wanted, and were no longer dependent on the TV programmers to schedule our favorite episodes.

But despite immense popularity, the DVDs did face some controversy. With the release of the sixth season, gone was the classic cardboard box we were used to with the previous releases, and we were instead met with a plastic case in the shape of Homer's head.

The clamshell style was universally despised by collectors and caused instant uproar online. *Simpsons* message boards were clogged with posts complaining about the new design. A lot of this anger stemmed from the drastic change of theme, from a cardboard box set with the Simpsons family sitting on their couch. The choice to have this as a plastic case in the shape of Homer's head instead made this stick out like a sore thumb on DVD shelves.

The material was also flimsy, and easy to break. The case would refuse to remain shut, forcing many to tape it closed. Due to a thin ridge at the bottom, it couldn't even stand up on its own, so it had to be pressed between other DVD cases to stop it falling down.

FOX anticipated the backlash by prepacking the set with a flyer. This flyer directed the buyer to a website where they could purchase a cardboard box for $2.95 US or $4.95 CA shipping. The flyer contained the show's typical snarky humor, poking fun at fans who purchased the DVDs:

Following the backlash, FOX attempted to fix this mistake for the UK release by announcing that the Homer head would be a limited edition and only 50,000 would be released. Copies of the alternative box began arriving in the USA in late 2005. But this still wasn't good enough for some fans, as the new design didn't include the *Simpsons* signature couch, and instead showed Homer with a magnifying glass. From this point on, all covers featured one primary character, instead of the whole Simpsons family.

Having learned from their mistake, the following seasons were released in the cardboard box, as well as the plastic head, allowing fans to choose which design they wanted. The seventh season was Marge's head, the eighth season was Maggie's, the next was Lisa's, and season ten was Bart.

However, just when some fans had finally embraced the clamshell plastic head, the creators decided to change it yet again. The eleventh season release was a hybrid design of Krusty the Clown's head. While the previous five yellow clamshell designs were shaped like the characters' respective heads, season eleven was the standard box with the 3D facial features of the clam-case.

The DVD box sets were released each subsequent year. But that all changed after the release of the twelfth season in 2009, instead jumping straight to season twenty and bypassing the seven other seasons before it. This was to coincide with the twentieth anniversary of the show. This naturally rubbed fans the wrong way, as some feared at the time that they would be left with an incomplete collection.

But those fears were put to rest only a few days later, when the thirteenth season was released on September 20.

This was followed by season fourteen the following year, all the way to sixteen in 2013. However, in 2015, Al Jean suddenly announced that The Simpsons would no longer see home media releases. This was due to dwindling DVD sales, combined with the rise of streaming services and downloads. Another factor was the rising popularity of the cable channel FXX and its reruns, and FOX's on-demand video service, FXNOW. What's worse was that these online services were only available to fans in the US, leaving a huge portion of Simpsons fans in other areas of the world left out.

When fans were finally resigned to the fact that they were going to have an empty space between their seventeenth and twentieth season DVD box sets, Al Jean made another huge announcement in July 2017. During a San Diego Comic Con panel, Jean stated that, due to fan demand, the eighteenth season DVD would be released after all, on December 5, 2017.

Two years later saw the release of the complete nineteenth season in December 2019. This was the final season released on DVD. And while many purists could finally complete their season one to twenty collection, there were still many more seasons that would never see a home media release. It seems as if the fans' impending sense of doom was sensed by the creators, because with season nineteen's DVD came another note—from Matt Groening himself:

A Plea For Sanity

Hello, long-suffering Simpsons devotees!

We know, we know. It's been several decades since the last Simpsons box, and many of you are ready to fling yourselves headfirst into Springfield Gorge, cursing our names all the way down.

But stop your raging despair right now! Step back from the ledge! Don't hurl yourselves!

Here ya go with a brand-new nostalgic package of shrink-wrapped entertainment in your favorite medium of yesteryear, the DVD. This season – 19, I guess – is one of the good ones. It's got Marge bonding with a sack of potatoes, Mr. Burns finding a penny in a water fountain, Maggie clipping her own toenails, Lisa almost smoking a cigarette, and Martin falling down a cliff.

But it's not all subtle observational comedy. We've also got the big, goofy, over-the-top knee-slappers you love: Bart befriends an alien and Marge and Homer become professional assassins in "Treehouse of Horror XVIII." Then there's our Emmy®-winning 409th episode, "Eternal Moonshine of the Simpson Mind," in which Homer can't remember the events of the previous night, with spooky, cosmic consequences. Plus you get "Funeral for a Fiend," in which Sideshow Bob [SPOILER ALERT! STOP READING NOW!] almost kills Bart again. And all 20 episodes are, as usual, festooned with ego-driven audio commentaries by us, the same schmoes who have been yammering at you for the last generation or two.

Guest stars include Stephen Colbert, Maya Rudolph, Glenn Close, Beverly D'Angelo, Zooey Deschanel, Jon Stewart, John C. Reilly, Julia Louis-Dreyfus, Lionel Richie, Terry Gross, Dan Rather, Jack Black, Plácido Domingo, the Dixie Chicks, and many, many more. At least, many more. OK, a few more.

As always, this whole shebang is brought to you by the mobs of animators, actors, writers, producers, musicians, and executives who make the show happen. On behalf of all of us, we thank you, the loyal, neglected fans, for your fervid, almost obsessive, devotion over the years.

And when is the next DVD box coming, you ask? I can confidently assure you: Someday!

Your binge-watching amigo,

MATT GROENING

Although it was a bittersweet ending for DVD collectors, the nineteenth season's inner sleeve had incredible artwork by Bill Plympton, the artist behind some of *The Simpsons*'s most creative and beautiful Couch Gags. The artwork showed the family on a bizarre and wild road trip, surrounded by dinosaurs, which then ventured under the sea. These illustrations were also beautifully animated for the DVD menu screen and accompanied by a soothing rendition of the theme song, composed by James Dooley.

Al Jean has teased in the past that, if and when the show ended, they would consider a special set for collectors. But, seeing as the show continues to be greenlit for many more seasons to come, don't expect that to happen anytime soon.

The decision to discontinue DVDs remains a controversial one amongst fans. We cannot deny that, as with the downfall of VHS, accessibility, cost, and ease of use are huge factors in the turning over of technology. So streaming became the new normal for home entertainment, and the DVD shelves were shrinking in homes and growing only in Goodwill stores.

The Simpsons Moves to Streaming

In March 2019, Disney's deal to buy FOX was finalized, and as such, *The Simpsons* was now under the ownership of the House of Mouse—which we're sure was a little awkward for the creators, after decades of jokes and jibes at Disney's expense.

The biggest reason for Disney acquiring FOX was its huge library of content, a vast well of iconic movies and television shows, including, of course, our yellow family of five.

That same year, in November 2019, Disney+ was released in the States, a service that many people were hugely anticipating. The first thirty seasons of *The Simpsons* came with it, available to watch at the click of a button. Season thirty-one was added on October 2, 2020, and season thirty-two on September 29, 2021, in the United States. By this point, much of the rest of the world now had access to the service. Although many diehard collectors lamented the end of the DVD releases, the response to the move to Disney+ was massively welcomed from people across the world.

The Simpsons continues to be one of Disney+'s best performing shows, becoming the most-watched television show in 2021 on Disney+ worldwide. That is an incredible feat when you consider that massively popular exclusives like Star Wars's *The Mandalorian* and Marvel's *Wanda Vision* were also released that year.

It seemed that the service not only allowed old fans to relive the show, it also let new people be introduced to it for the first time. It also allowed many lapsed older fans, who had stopped watching the show around its earlier seasons, to see what they'd been missing. It also relayed the show to the next generation, with parents showing their children the adventures of Springfield.

Despite its popularity, however, there was controversy almost instantly. Disney released *The Simpsons* in upscaled full HD, instead of its original 4:3 aspect ratio. This meant that the images were stretched to fill the entire screen. As such, some classic visual gags were simply cropped out. For example, Bart's prank involving a balloon of Skinner holding a sign that reads, "Hi! I'm Big Butt Skinner" had Skinner's large bottom cropped out. One other notable example was from the season four episode, "Duffless." In a great visual gag, it showed Duff—from Duff Lite to Duff Dry—being produced from the exact same pipe. But the joke is completely lost with the cropped 16:9 version, causing all physical media purists to lean back and laugh that their DVDs were correctly scaled in 4:3 by default.

Following the backlash, producer Al Jean announced that the show would soon be available to view in its original 4:3 aspect ratio beginning May 28.

Aside from this hiccup, there are other downfalls to being an online library only. As home media enthusiasts can attest, once you purchase a DVD or Blu-ray, that is yours to own forever (unless your mother sold all your DVDs in a garage sale, like mine did!). So, should a streaming service decide to remove content from their online library, you can at least still watch the DVD anytime you want.

A recent example of this was in 2022. Following the merger of Warner and Discovery in 2022, HBO Max announced that many shows would be taken off their platform. This was apparently a cost-saving method to minimize their debt and write down axed shows as a tax write-off. As such, some beloved television shows would not be available to watch legally anywhere online. Some of the creators of the canceled shows even actively encouraged their fans to download the show any way they could. (Cut to me donning a pirate hat.)

While the risk of this happening to such a cultural-icon show as *The Simpsons* is unlikely, it does highlight the potential downside to exclusive streaming apps. Although it is safe to assume that *The Simpsons* as a whole is a safe commodity on Disney+, some episodes are notably absent in some countries.

For example, Hong Kong's Disney+ does not have the season sixteen episode, "Goo Goo Gai Pan." The episode was quietly removed, as authorities in Hong Kong clamped down on banning content that violated a strict national security law. The episode in question featured a reference to the iconic "Tank Man" photo. In the same episode, the family came across a plaque at Tiananmen Square in Beijing that read: "On this site, in 1989, nothing happened." The removal of this episode has raised concerns about media censorship.

Another classic episode that was removed much closer to home is season three's, "Stark Raving Dad," which is nowhere to be found. Many fans across the world have been vocal about the absence of this classic episode, especially as it contained one of the catchiest songs in the entire show, "Lisa, It's Your Birthday."

Although many blamed this on Disney, it was actually a decision made by the *Simpsons* team before the acquisition. The removal of this episode was in response to a documentary that contained many disturbing allegations against Michael Jackson.

Producer Al Jean explained: "I'm against book-burning of any kind. But this is our book, and we're allowed to take out a chapter."

Slate journalist Isaac Butler criticized the removal as "an offense against art and the medium of television, and part of a growing trend of corporations using their consolidated power and the death of physical media to do damage control by destroying works by troublesome artists."

In addition to raising concerns about censorship, many fans have lamented the lack of bonus content on Disney+. Almost all of the extra features found on the DVDs, like the audio commentaries for instance, were notably absent. Many of you reading this surely agree that the commentaries were the highlight of the DVDs. Their main appeal was getting closer to the show, and this feature allowed us to get to know the writers, directors, and voice artists a lot more. It gave us another perspective on the episodes, that I think would be so important to look back on when remembering *The Simpsons*–as a bonus, they were freaking hilarious!

Closing Thoughts

As collectors, we can only hope that, if and when the show ends, the creators will release a DVD or Blu-ray box set of the complete series. It is a show that furthers TV programmers, corporate contracts, and profit margins. It should be celebrated with permanence so that, should your child or grandchild hold up a disc in wonder at what these weird little yellow creatures were, you can slot it into your disc-drive and wake up the world of Springfield once more.

CHAPTER FOUR
Books

WARREN EVANS

It should come as no surprise that in addition to toys, hair gel, cookie jars, comics, and board games, there would also be plenty of *Simpsons* books. This includes everything from Bart explaining his approach to life, to Springfield travel guides, all the way to *The Simpsons* being used (unofficially) as an exercise in studying philosophy. Most of us at one point or another have enjoyed books. I mean, you're even reading a book right now! I will use this chapter to put a spotlight on some of the more memorable offerings.

One of the earliest and best examples of them using this space is the book adaptation of the first aired full-length episode, "Simpsons Roasting on an Open Fire," entitled *The Simpsons Xmas Book*.

This is a clever approach, especially with an episode this popular, since most of the images used are directly taken from the show, giving you an extra way of following along with this Christmas classic.

It's after the release of this book that we saw them start to settle further into a style that really sets the books apart from other merchandise. This was done by treating the books as if they were made by the family themselves, a move that still makes them feel special, over thirty years later. *The Simpsons Uncensored Family Album* was a step directly into the life of the family off camera.

This also is where we start to see the humor translated very well to another medium, with the book assembled almost like a scrapbook—littered with handwritten notes, photographs, letters from the hospital after Bart was born, newspaper clippings, and even a report card for Santa's Little Helper. The back cover makes this claim as if it were written by Bart himself:

"NOTHING OMITTED! NO PUNCHES PULLED! ASSEMBLED AND NARRATED WITH PAINSTAKING, LOVING CARE BY NONE OTHER THAN THAT FIRST LADY OF TALL HAIR, MARGE SIMPSON. YOU'LL LAUGH! YOU'LL CRY! YOU'LL TURN THE PAGE!"

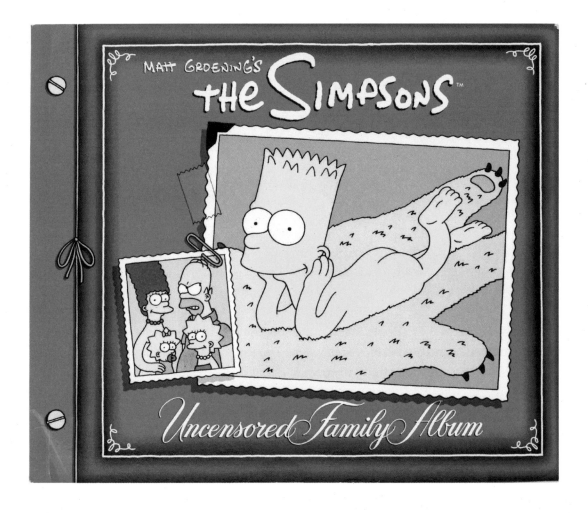

If this book makes one thing clear, it's that *The Simpsons* always had a knack for marketing and finding new ways to use the license. In addition to creating a fictional scrapbook, the team capitalized on the fun design of these characters further by way of "Fun Book" activities such as puzzles, cut-out decorations for your bike, and game concepts for you and your friends. (There's even a spitball dart board.) This concept gave us the *Rainy Day Fun Book*, as well as the *Fun in the Sun Book*.

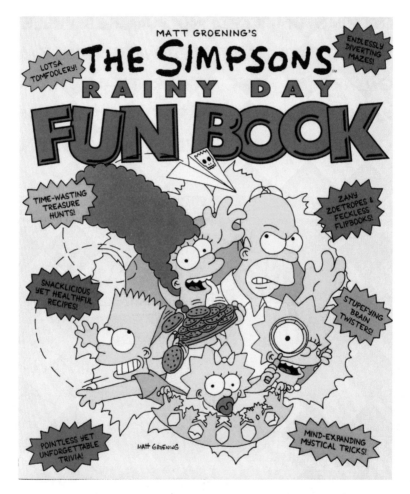

What really makes these books stand out is that they quite literally encouraged you to turn off the TV and go outside—ironic, since *The Simpsons* is a TV show—or use your brain by figuring out one of the many games within. This not only distracted you from staring at the "idiot box," but it focused your attention fully on *Simpsons*-themed activities, and with plenty of bright colors and fantastic designs along the way. You could make your own zoetrope, or even learn how to make a balloon inflate itself! (With adult supervision, naturally.)

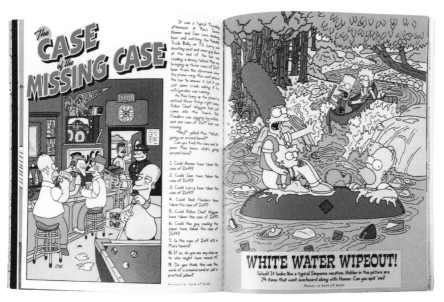

With that said, if there is one book being discussed here that strikes a special chord with so many fans, it is *Bart Simpson's Guide to Life: A Wee Handbook for the Perplexed*, released in 1993 by HarperCollins. Not only is this one packed with amazing drawings and great jokes, but much like the *Uncensored Family Album*, it really felt true to Bart's voice, and allowed kids to feel that extra connection to one of their favorite characters. Not only was it funny, but it felt "made for you."

The book set itself up perfectly with this quote from Bart on the back:

"STARVED FOR THE WHOLE TRUTH, MAN? TAKE A BITE OUT OF THIS BITSY BUT BEEFY PACKAGE, BRIMMING WITH FLAVORIZED MORSELS OF WIT, WISDOM, AND WORLDLY KNOWLEDGE BROUGHT TO YOU BY THE ONE AND ONLY BARTHOLOMEW J. SIMPSON ~ GET THE HARD-KNOCKS FACTS OF LIFE FROM THE GUY WHO'S SEEN IT ALL, HEARD IT ALL, DONE IT ALL ~ AND DENIES IT ALL."

The jokes start instantly with this fake disclaimer on page one:

"DISCLAIMER: THIS BOOK HAS BEEN CREATED SOLELY FOR ENTERTAINMENT PURPOSES. I, BART SIMPSON, TAKE FULL CREDIT FOR ALL IMPROVEMENTS IN YOUR LIFE COMMENCING AS OF YOUR PURCHASE OF THIS BOOK AND CONTINUING FOR A REASONABLE PERIOD OF TIME THEREAFTER OR UNTIL HELL FREEZES OVER, WHICHEVER IS LONGER. I, BART SIMPSON, ACCEPT NO BLAME FOR ANY TROUBLE YOU MIGHT GET INTO BECAUSE OF SAME, INCLUDING BUT NOT LIMITED TO; GROUNDING, DETENTION, EXPULSION FROM SCHOOL, DISFIGURING HUNTING ACCIDENTS, AND THE DEATH PENALTY. YOU HAVE NOW BEEN DULY WARNED. ENJOY!"

This life guide is something I'd recommend to any *Simpsons* fan. It covers everything from how to gross out your family at the dinner table, the many lies your parents tell you, how to get out of fights with bullies, all the way to how to annoy your Sunday school teacher, and my personal favorite: Heaven vs. Hell—which is better? This book captures Bart as perfectly as ever.

This book not only focused on Bart, but gave us small glimpses into other members of the family. A few favorites of mine include the back-to-back "Dream Room" spreads from both Lisa and Bart, as well as Beauty Secrets from Homer, "The Swami of Swank," and Marge, "The Goddess of Glamour." Both are clearly worthy of taking notes.

Much like *Simpsons Illustrated* and *Simpsons Comics*, these books were a fun way to use the bright colors and unique style of the show to make completely original situations and images. Handled by a lot of the same people who went on to start and work on *Simpsons Comics*, one could say these were the perfect warm-ups.

BART SIMPSON'S

Guide to Life

A wee handbook for the perplexed

Helped into print by Matt Groening

Within the same year, we also got *Cartooning with The Simpsons: Hot Tips 'n' Tricks From The Master Doodler Matt Groening.* This drawing guide showed any curious fan exactly how to figure out the proportions when drawing their favorite characters from the show. Tips like "Bart's basic head shape is a cylinder, kinda like a tin can" and "Think of Homer's hair as two croquet hoops," along with the actual step-by-step process of drawing them, make this book extremely fun and useful.

As a kid, I always struggled to get the height of Bart's head right, or size the eyeballs correctly to the rest of Homer's face. This guide really broke it down in a way that had you making convincing knockoffs in no time. It even gave you examples of the family all together, as well as an entire spread of the different hands and feet. There is an important sharing of credit on the final page, where they mention several key members of both the show and beyond:

"When David Silverman was first hired to help animate *The Simpsons*, he assumed the job would last three weeks. Six years later, he is a supervising director for the series. Wes Archer, one of the other original *Simpsons* animators, has directed many episodes. The two of them are largely responsible for the show's look and the way the characters move. Together, they helped develop the bible on how to draw the Simpsons, and a lot of the ideas in this book come from their notes.

Thanks go to Cindy and Steve Vance, who conceived and created this book, and to Bill Morrison, who did most of the actual drawings. And special thanks to everyone who has ever rendered the Simpsons professionally: cartoonists, graphic designers, costume makers, video game programmers, toy figurine sculptors, giant parade-balloon inflators, and—oh yes—animators."

With a similar idea in mind, fourteen years later, we got *The Simpsons Handbook,* except this time they expanded on the family, and included tons of other characters like Moe, Principal Skinner, Ralph Wiggum, Otto, and many more. They also did an entire section on costume changes and backgrounds, giving a bit more of a glimpse into the details in comparison to its 1993 predecessor. This book included work from a multitude of artists, from the comics as well as the animation team.

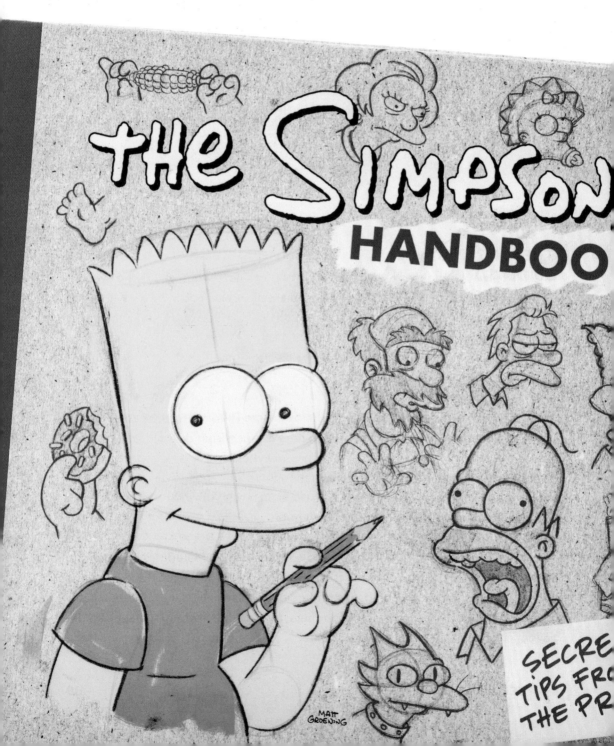

By 1997, the show had been around long enough to realize how much the fans loved the tiny details, the bits of knowledge that made us feel like even bigger fans. We had fully accepted that the Simpsons had set up camp in our heads, and weren't going anywhere. With this, the show made good use of that information in the form of the first Episode Guide.

There were initially four of these guides:

THE SIMPSONS: A COMPLETE GUIDE TO OUR FAVORITE FAMILY (1997). SEASONS ONE TO EIGHT

THE SIMPSONS FOREVER!: A COMPLETE GUIDE TO OUR FAVORITE FAMILY...CONTINUED (1999). SEASONS NINE TO TEN

THE SIMPSONS BEYOND FOREVER! A COMPLETE GUIDE TO OUR FAVORITE FAMILY...STILL CONTINUED (2002). SEASONS ELEVEN TO TWELVE

THE SIMPSONS ONE STEP BEYOND FOREVER!: A COMPLETE GUIDE TO OUR FAVORITE FAMILY...CONTINUED YET AGAIN (2005). SEASONS THIRTEEN TO FOURTEEN

These guides were an episode-by-episode look at all the things we love about the show, but also with a focus on things you might miss or forget. Each one provides not only a synopsis, and the writer's and director's names, but the chalkboard gag and the best jokes. One page might give you a bio of Krusty the Clown, or the lyrics to the Itchy & Scratchy theme song. These books were made with lots of love and gave you a serious leg up in *Simpsons* trivia.

For instance, did you know the chalkboard gag for "Krusty Gets Kancelled" was "I will not charge admission to the bathroom"? Or that the song Bart, Nelson, Milhouse, and Martin listen to while in the car in *Bart On the Road* is "Radar Love" by Golden Earring? What about the fact that there is a medieval mace and a green knit cap in Jimbo's locker in "Lisa's Date With Density"? These are the kinds of things that make these books beloved by fans still.

Sliding back a few years, we arrive at another memorable one: *The Simpsons Guide to Springfield*. As the name suggests, this is meant to act as a travel guide, highlighting all the many things to do around Springfield.

"Home of the Isotopes, Springfield A&M, and Blinky, the world's first three-eyed fish! Birthplace of the Flaming Moe! The sight of Krustylu Studios, the awe-inspiring Springfield Gorge, and a world-renowned box factory! O Springfield! What many wonders you offer up for our consumption!"

"YES, WE'VE ALL HEARD SPRINGFIELD CALLED THE COUNTRY'S "WORST CITY" AND "AMERICA'S CRUDBUCKET." BUT IS IT ALL THAT BAD? WELL, MAYBE YES AND MAYBE NO—YOU BE THE JUDGE!"

Like the other books discussed here, this one is full of fun images, like Troy McClure shoving his hands in wet cement in front of the Aztec Theater, and Krusty dunking on Ned Flanders at the local Springfield Two-Man Interfaith Jammy-Jam. It is also organized with great attention, keeping it very much in the tone of a travel guide.

We see a lot covered here: Attractions, Lodging, Dining, Shopping, Annual Events, and even a survival Guide.

We also get the following essays:

COME FOR THE FUN, STAY FOR THE GUILT: A VACATIONER'S GUIDE FOR WORSHIPING IN SPRINGFIELD BY REV. TIMOTHY LOVEJOY

SWINGIN' SPRINGFIELD: A BACHELOR'S GUIDE TO MY FAVORITE TOWN BY KIRK VAN HOUTEN

EVERYBODY INTO THE COOL: A KID'S GUIDE TO SPRINGFIELD BY BART SIMPSON

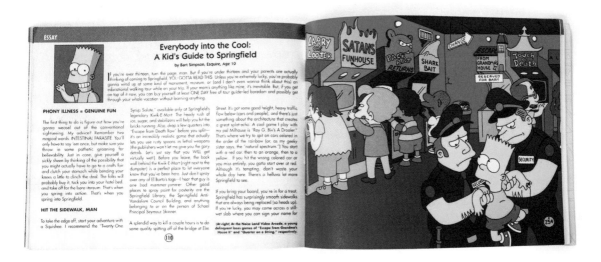

If learning more about individual characters is your thing, especially beyond the family, it doesn't get much better than *The Simpsons Library of Wisdom*. This series started in 2004 and ended in 2010, with ten books released in total. Each one features the character's top forty things, as well as their bottom forty. For example, Lisa mentions "extended sax solos," "Mom's pancakes," and "TV commercials with raccoons in them" in her top forty. She mentions "global warming," "mistaking stubbornness for character," and "the grim truth that we can't all just get along" in her bottom forty. It also featured things like a mini-mystery written by Lisa, a Family Vacation Cringe Index, and Lisa's Television Viewing Log.

Other books in this series include:

- **THE BART BOOK (2004)**

- **THE HOMER BOOK (2004)**

- **THE RALPH WIGGUM BOOK (2005)**

- **THE LISA BOOK (2006)**

- **THE KRUSTY BOOK (2006)**

- **FLANDERS' BOOK OF FAITH (2008)**

This sort of thing ties directly back to those early concepts. *Bart Simpson's Guide To Life* was a hit because it made us feel closer to the character, as if he actually wrote that book for us. This series connected us further to the universe and made some of the other Springfield staples feel equally real, in a way that maybe the show couldn't always do. Who doesn't want to read a book "written" by Ralph? I have a feeling all of you do.

The Simpsons Library of Wisdom

Closing Thoughts

As with most things throughout these chapters, we have tried our best to show just how far the show reached beyond the screen. Also, like other topics within this book, we could easily make an entire book about the books. Man, that's a lot of books—but it's the truth!

I think in general, the books are another perfect example of what this whole project is about, because they essentially represent the other side of the coin. When Matt created these characters, no one thought we'd still be talking about them over thirty years later. Not only did the show lead to clothing, toys, comics, and so many other tangible things—it led to very direct stories and ideas from the characters. Stories that felt real, like Bart and Lisa had book deals of their own. You have to imagine that this was key to the connection many of us formed to these characters. It's one thing to watch them on TV, but it's something else when you can carry a piece of that universe around in your backpack, or read it on the bus.

These are some of the many reasons why *The Simpsons* is still being made today. We didn't just watch the show and laugh—it was more than the jokes we ran to the kitchen to horribly retell to our mom so that she could give us a pity laugh. (Thanks, Mom.) *The Simpsons* found a way to exist with us, on our shirts, in the kitchen, next to the toothpaste, and even on the bookshelf. I'm so glad they did.

CHAPTER FIVE

Comics

JAMES HICKS

You may find it interesting to learn that, long before *The Simpsons* was a household name, Matt Groening was a struggling cartoonist who released his frustrations in the form of a comic strip entitled *Life in Hell*. This dark-comedic graphic literature focused on love, sex, work, and death, as well as exploring themes of angst, social alienation, self-loathing, and fear of inevitable doom—all through characters who took the form of anthropomorphic rabbits.

Groening photocopied and sold these zines for two dollars each at Licorice Pizza, the record store in which he worked on Sunset Boulevard. These humble photocopies were packed with comic strips, comedy sketches, letters, and photo collages. Groening also took great care with the covers. The first issue saw Binky, a rabbit-humanoid character, standing in a cloud of smog and declaring, "What you see is what you breathe." As well as humor with a dark edge, Groening also worked real photos into the covers, including drawings from Jules Verne's books and a picture of his family's living room. The use of personal imagery was not by accident—Groening based many of his early works on his experiences living and working in Los Angeles.

Although Groening originally self-published *Life in Hell*, the strip was picked up by *WET* magazine and later the *Los Angeles Reader* in 1980, which ran the strip weekly. In the mid-'80s, Groening's then-girlfriend, Deborah Caplan, helped publish a compilation of Groening's cartoons as a book.

Life in Hell eventually caught the attention of Hollywood producer James L. Brooks, who received one strip, "The Los Angeles Way of Death," as a gift from fellow producer Polly Platt. In 1985, Brooks contacted Groening with the proposition to develop a series of short, animated skits, called "bumpers," for *The Tracey Ullman Show*, originally envisioning a *Life in Hell* adaptation. But, fearing the loss of ownership rights to his beloved comic strip, Groening instead created an entirely new batch of characters:

Homer, Marge, Bart, Lisa, and Maggie Simpson. All but one was named after a member of his family, an indication that, like *Life in Hell,* these characters were hugely personal to Groening, but would also be hugely relatable. With each character came a definitive identity, and it became apparent that we all knew someone who shared a trait with one of these strange, yellow characters… and so, *The Simpsons* took over the world.

I believe the story of how Matt Groening got his start through his love and talent for comics sets the stage for how *Simpsons Comics* became globally successful in its own right. His experience with *Life in Hell* made him truly value this art of storytelling, and in a lot of ways, gave him more creative freedom than the televised version of the show. Like *Life in Hell*, Groening's *Simpsons Comics* experimented with stories, themes, formats, and artworks likely to be dismissed by mass media.

For twenty-five years, fans all over the world loved these comics, up until 2018 when production ended. If not for collectors like you, me, and probably your local Comic Book Guy, their stories would never be told or enjoyed ever again.

Therefore, I think it is incredibly important that we discuss…

WHOA MAMA! BIG PREMIERE ISSUE!

SIMPSONS
ILLUSTRATED

I WILL NOT READ THIS MAGAZINE IN CLASS
I WILL NOT READ THIS MAGAZINE IN CLASS
I WILL NOT READ THIS MAGA   ASS
I WILL NOT READ THIS MAG·   S
I WILL NOT READ THIS MAG
I WILL NOT READ THIS MA·
I WILL NOT READ THIS M·
I WILL NOT READ THIS
I WILL NOT READ T·
I WILL NOT READ T·
I WILL NOT READ
I WILL NOT READ T·
I WILL NOT READ   ·SS
I WILL NOT READ   S
I WILL NOT READ   .ASS
I WILL NOT READ THIS M   .ASS
I WILL NOT READ THIS MAG.   ASS
I WILL NOT READ THIS MAGA   SS
I WILL NOT READ THIS MAG
I WILL N·

SECRETS REVEALED!
GIANT FOLDOUT GUIDE TO
THE SIMPSONS' UNIVERSE!

STARTLING EXPOSÉ!
THE TERRIBLE TRUTH
ABOUT GOLDILOCKS!

BACKSTAGE EXCLUSIVE!
AN INTERVIEW WITH TOP
SIMPSON ANIMATORS!

MATT
GROENING
© TM TWENTIETH CENTURY FOX FILM CORP. ALL RIGHTS RESERVED

SPECIAL PULLOUT BONUS ! YOUR VERY OWN COPY OF
THE SPRINGFIELD SHOPPER
NEWSPAPER INSIDE THIS ISSUE!

$2.50   SPRING 1991

Simpsons Illustrated

James L. Brooks accepted the Simpsons family into *The Tracey Ullman Show*, in 1987, and the first official *Simpsons* short, "Good Night" was broadcast across America. But Matt Groening was not only a talented cartoonist, but also a shrewd businessman. While initially negotiating with FOX, Groening requested the publishing rights to the show, and not realizing what a commodity they had on their hands, FOX agreed.

This is similar to what George Lucas did with Star Wars, where FOX agreed to let him have the merchandise rights.

As *The Simpsons* ran as a bumper on *The Tracy Ullman Show*, the yellow family started to overshadow the host herself. Yes, the animation style was slightly crude, because of its low budget, but the family was so memorable that they were eventually given their very own prime-time show, with the first episode, "Simpsons Roasting on an Open Fire," broadcast in 1989. The show was a huge success, with viewership in the tens of millions, during its first couple of seasons.

With *The Simpsons* dominating the small screen, Matt Groening decided to expand the show into familiar territory by launching *Simpsons Illustrated* in 1991.

Simpsons Illustrated was a companion magazine to the show produced by Matt Groening, Bill Morrison, and Cindy and Steve Vance, with Katy Dobbs as the editorial director. The first issue was released on April 4, 1991, and it was packed with amazing details and thoughtful features. It contained a copy of the *Springfield Shopper*, a fold-out poster outlining every character from the show (and their relationship to each other), and an original bedtime story by Bart, along with an *Official Simpsons Illustrated School Survival Handbook*, which shared Bart's classroom tactical tips, guerrilla strategies, and a diagram displaying the best seat in class. It ran for ten issues, from 1991 to 1993, and featured articles, interviews with the cast and crew, artworks by fans, and one of the most popular sections…the comic strip!

These strips were written and drawn mostly by Steve Vance and Bill Morrison. Fans absolutely loved the comic strip, and it was one of the biggest things they looked forward to in the next issue. The overwhelming success of the comic strips led to the expansion of them in the issues. In our interview with Morrison, he explained: "The comics started expanding to two pages to five pages, and ultimately ten and twelve. We were having more fun with the comics than any other part of the magazine."

This enthusiasm for the comics led to a one-shot comic edition titled *Simpsons Comics and Stories*. This issue was entirely dedicated to the comics, and its popularity was the reason why Bongo Comics Group was created in 1993.

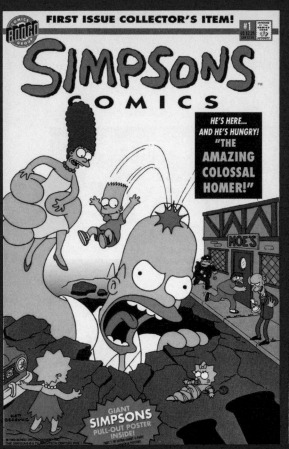

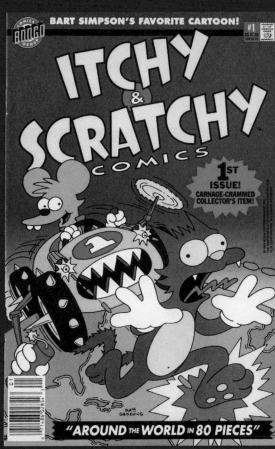

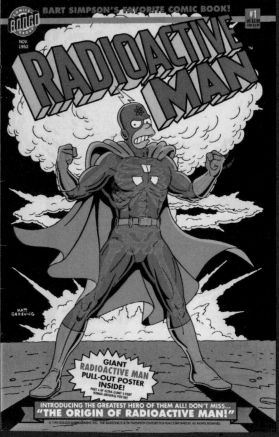

Bongo Comics Group

"THERE ARE THINGS YOU CAN DO IN THE COMICS YOU COULDN'T DO ON TV BECAUSE THE READER CONTROLS THE RATE THE STORY MOVES AT, AND THEY CAN TAKE A MOMENT TO LET THE ART SINK IN."

—IAN BOOTHBY, THE SIMPSONS COMIC WRITER

The name "Bongo" came from Groening's bunny character from his aforementioned comic, *Life in Hell*. It was a comic book publishing company founded by Matt Groening, Steve and Cindy Vance, and Bill Morrison.

Matt's idea for the company was to create more "fun" and lighthearted comics, which he felt was lacking at the time. "I go into comic book stores and look at all the stuff, and, for the most part, it looks like fairly grim science-fiction and superhero stuff…I guess I just thought there was room out there for funny comic books."

The company launched four titles in late 1993 alone: *Bartman, Itchy & Scratchy, Radioactive Man*, and of course, the more traditional *Simpsons Comics*.

The very first issue started with a bang (quite literally). "The Amazing Colossal Homer" saw Homer zapped by Mr. Burns and transformed into a colossal giant. And, like Homer's butt, the issue's success was huge! It became one of the highest-selling comics in its debut month and the team even won an Eisner Award for it!

Much like the television show, the comics made great use of parody—taking iconic comic covers and paying homage to them, with "The Amazing Colossal Homer" being a direct parody of *Fantastic Four* issue #1 from 1961. This was because of the Bongo team's deep love of superhero comics.

Bill Morrison said of this project: "We were all comic book fans and saw the comic version of *The Simpsons* as a perfect vehicle to parody covers and stories of comics. We knew our readers would relate to them in a way that the mainstream TV audience might not. It started in the very beginning when we were just starting to plan the early Bongo books. Steve Vance, who was the editor and writer, asked me to come up with some promotional images that would be distributed to retailers as posters and other promo items. He wanted classic comic cover parodies that retailers and comic fans would relate to. So I sketched up a handful of ideas based on covers like *Avengers* #4, *Captain America* #111, etc. One of them was a parody of the iconic cover of *FF* #1. Steve loved the sketch so much that he decided we should make it the cover of *Simpsons Comics* #1, and wrote the main story for that issue based on it."

COLLECTING THE SIMPSONS

These first issues of *Simpsons Comics* were released a few months apart, until issue #6, when the comic became a monthly publication. Despite a team much smaller than the show's, the level of quality within each issue was impressive. Moreover, instead of going the easy route by reusing and adapting TV episodes, Morrison and his team created their own original story lines. Not only this, but they made them feel authentic to the show. Morrison again: "I made sure the comics were so close to the show. So that people accepted them as part of that continuity. As we paid very close attention to changes in the show. So if a character dies like Maude Flanders or if they retire a character, I will make sure they disappear from the comic."

The comics closely tracked the continuity further than character disappearances. When Lisa became a vegetarian in season seven's "Lisa the Vegetarian," Paul McCartney requested that she maintain this throughout the rest of the series. This was part of his stipulation of being a guest on the show. Therefore, Bill made it his due diligence to see that Lisa was never shown eating meat in the comics. In maintaining such a close connection between the two mediums, it felt more seamless switching from the television show to the comics. In fact, Morrison recalls some fans getting confused between issues of the comics, and actual episodes: "Every so often people would come up and talk about an issue of the comic book, as one of their favorite episodes. Not realizing that they were not talking about the comic. That was the best compliment I could get."

This was one of the many reasons why the comics were so popular. Having content that was written with such care for the show's continuity, as well as its general authenticity, allowed fans to seamlessly keep up with the Simpsons family, not only between weekly television episodes, but also when the show went into hiatus over the summer.

The comics were so entwined with the show that they even expanded further on certain one-time jokes or characters, such as in issue #45, where we were graced with the return of Mr. Sparkle in "Mr. Sparkle: Destroy all Manga!" Here, the Japanese soap mascot fights with Goku from *Dragon Ball Z,* as well as Pikachu…or, as Mr. Sparkle says, "Pikkanoze."

Even fan favorite Hank Scorpio popped up a few times in the comics, like #243 which expanded on his friendship with Homer.

Although Matt Groening gave the mandate that the comics should be as close to the show as possible, they also realized that you can experiment with comics far more than you could with TV. With the concept of the multiverse going very far back in comic book

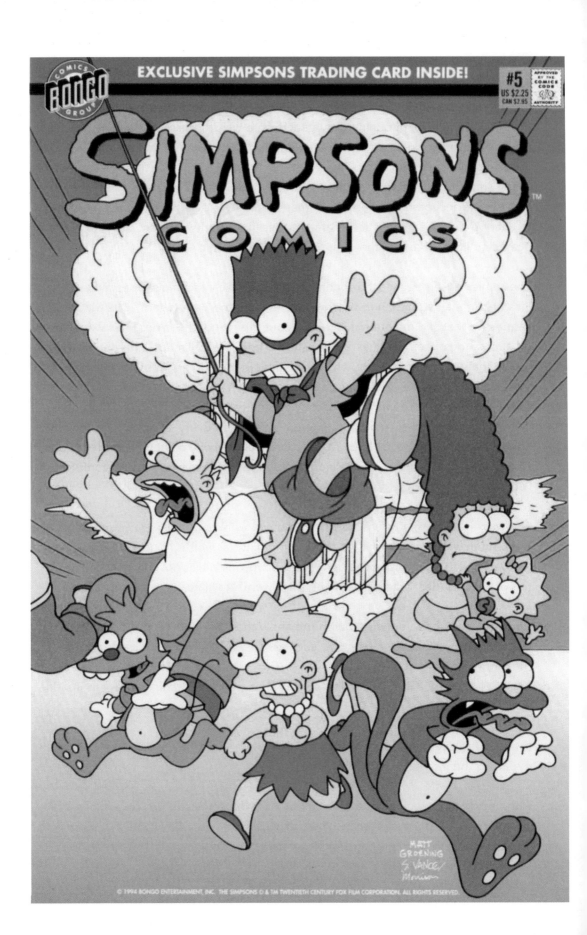

lore, the writers played with this idea when they created the "metaverse" in #5, "When Bongos Collide." In this awesome issue, we see the Simpsons come face to face with Bartman, Itchy and Scratchy, and Kang and Kodos, in the crossover of the century. It was ridiculously fun, and a concept we could never imagine being on TV.

Aside from the more fantastical storylines, Bongo Comics also dealt with topics such as free speech and creative ownership. One example is the story "Give Me Merchandising Or Give Me Death" in #13, written by Gary Glasberg, who would go on to become the showrunner of CBS's *NCIS*.

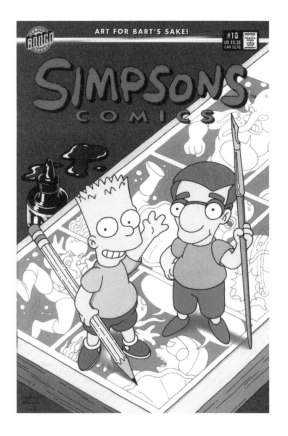

The comic saw Bart and Milhouse create their own comic, *Oyster Man*. When the boys present their idea, they are instantly dismissed by the industry pros, and told their work "sucks." But they are shocked to find that the same professionals stole their idea and are making billions of dollars from it. If that's not bad enough, the company then hires the boys and underpays them. This was a very real commentary on the truths of corporate greed, and hinted at the personal grievances of writers and artists and how they are treated in the industry—a topic that is timeless, and therefore oh so quintessentially *Simpsons*.

Radioactive Man

Aside from the main *Simpsons Comics*, Bongo released many other tie-ins. These included 1993's previously discussed *Bartman* and *Itchy and Scratchy,* as well as the hugely popular *Radioactive Man*. These issues gave fans the chance to peek more into the fictional world *inside* the fictional world of Springfield.

The way it was released was as unique as its humor. The second issue, released in March 1994, was titled *Radioactive Man* #88, the third issue was #216, followed by #412, then #679, before jumping all the way to #1,000. Although it would ordinarily take a few decades for a comic book series to reach this huge milestone, *Radioactive Man* accomplished this feat in only six issues, spanning from 1993 to 1994.

Having the *Radioactive Man* issues leap forward in issue numbers was to create this fictional impression that he was one of the oldest and longest-running comic book superheroes. It also allowed them to make jokes and use tropes based on the many different eras of comics the writers grew up reading. These issues also usually gave a fictional release date, really lending themselves to those tropes. A lot of the *Radioactive Man* covers were direct references to classic comic book imagery, like issue #412 being a recreation of *Batman*'s *A Death in The Family*, and #1,000 being a reference to *Spawn*.

Bill Morrison says, "That was Steve's [Vance] idea. Since *Radioactive Man* was a six-issue mini-series, he wanted it to span five decades and have a thread running through each self-contained story that connected them all. Steve wanted the sixth issue to be #1,000, so he even made an imaginary publishing chart so he could figure out how to make the sixth issue #1,000, given that #1 was set in 1952. At one point in the '80s, RM was supposedly coming out two or three times a week. The chart was also very useful in calculating what number the other issues should be."

Following this, Bongo released "new" issues that fell in random places among the timeline, which ran sporadically from the year 2000 to 2004. It was such a fun and creative idea, and felt very in keeping with *The Simpsons*'s meta humor.

Treehouse of Horror

One of the other most popular publications from Bongo Comics was the annual *The Simpsons' Treehouse of Horror*, formerly known as *Bart Simpson's Treehouse of Horror*. Inspired by the Halloween specials of the same name, they were released every year from 1995 all the way to 2017. The spooky specials have been a fan favorite since 1990, putting the family in bizarre and dangerous situations that you could never do in the regular episodes of the show. You could kill off main characters, or have Springfield obliterated by aliens, and everything would be back to the status quo by the next episode. The *Simpsons* writers loved writing the Treehouse specials because they were not tied down to the show's continuity, meaning that they could let loose and have fun.

Much like the TV show, the *Treehouse of Horror* comics gave the team free rein in terms of, not only violence, but creativity too. Bill Morrison, who illustrated some of the covers, was heavily inspired by the painted comic covers released by Marvel, and therefore wanted to replicate this with *The Simpsons*. "Everybody loved it, including Matt [Groening]. He said you need to do this more and invite other artists to come in and do their own styles. From that point on we started inviting artists."

Therefore, other talented artists joined in to contribute to the *Treehouse of Horror* comics, and Bill Morrison encouraged them to draw the Simpsons in their own unique style, which led to some truly stunning works.

There are so many great stories, and so much incredible art over its twenty-three-issue run, that it was quite frankly a daunting task to know what to focus on specifically. I feel like I am doing the series an injustice by not talking about each and every issue and story separately. But if I were to do that, then this would be less a coffee table book and more an actual table. But I will highlight a few standouts for me, such as "Ring Around the Simpsons" from issue #9. In a story from Ian Boothy, the Simpsons are transported to Middle-earth, where they meet the Fellowship of the Ring. Seeing Homer, Marge, Bart, and Lisa interacting with Frodo and Gandalf is both surreal and funny. We see Marge scorning Gandalf for "letting these children go barefoot in the snow," and Gandalf remarking that he "senses great evil" in Bart, who replies, "Yeah, yeah, I've heard it all before, Yoda." And seeing Homer defeat the mighty Balrog with a loud belch before accidentally knocking the Grey Wizard to his death is hilariously dark. Aside from the writing, what really makes this story stand out is the beautiful paintwork by artist Dan Brereton. It has a fantasy storybook feel that would look right at home in an official illustrated Tolkien novel, aside from the Simpsons breaking that illusion somewhat.

But one of my all-time favorite stories is "Murder He Wrote," from issue #14. Written by Ian Boothby and penciled by Nina Matsumoto, this parody of *Death Note* is drawn almost exactly like the manga, while at the same time feeling authentically *Simpsons*. Just like the original story, it opens with Bart finding a notebook that kills anyone that gets their name written into it. Krusty plays the role of Shinigami, and Lisa takes on the role of L, both excellent choices for their characters. The deaths are creatively gruesome, with Sideshow Bob first being attacked by a swarm of bees before falling face down into "boiling wiener water," and then getting flattened during the "annual steamroller parade."

Both Boothby and Matsumoto deservedly won an Eisner Award for their work. So I'd highly recommend you seek this one out and read it for yourself.

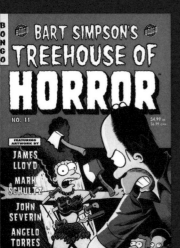

Futurama Crossover

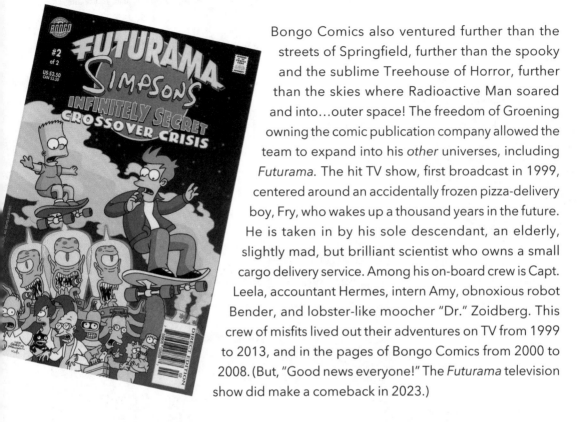

Bongo Comics also ventured further than the streets of Springfield, further than the spooky and the sublime Treehouse of Horror, further than the skies where Radioactive Man soared and into…outer space! The freedom of Groening owning the comic publication company allowed the team to expand into his *other* universes, including *Futurama.* The hit TV show, first broadcast in 1999, centered around an accidentally frozen pizza-delivery boy, Fry, who wakes up a thousand years in the future. He is taken in by his sole descendant, an elderly, slightly mad, but brilliant scientist who owns a small cargo delivery service. Among his on-board crew is Capt. Leela, accountant Hermes, intern Amy, obnoxious robot Bender, and lobster-like moocher "Dr." Zoidberg. This crew of misfits lived out their adventures on TV from 1999 to 2013, and in the pages of Bongo Comics from 2000 to 2008. (But, "Good news everyone!" The *Futurama* television show did make a comeback in 2023.)

In 2014, *The Simpsons* released the season twenty-six episode "Simpsonsrama." But this was not the first time Homer had met Bender. In January 2002, twelve years before the episode, the comic issue entitled *The Simpsons-Futurama Infinitely Secret Crossover Crisis #1* was released.

The first idea for crossing over these two Groening properties came from Morrison, who also worked on the *Futurama* show when it first started. He pitched the idea of the show crossover, but Matt was hesitant. "He [Groening] said no to the idea—he said that they are not in the same universe. But in my mind, *Futurama* is our universe…but 1,000 years from now. And *The Simpsons* is a fictional universe."

So Morrison and writer Ian Boothby went back to the drawing board to find a way to execute the idea

in a way that would appease Groening. Their new direction was inspired by the *Futurama* episode "The Day the Earth Stood Stupid," where the invading brain spawn transported Fry and the gang into the books *Moby Dick* and *Pride and Prejudice*. So, if they could be transported into books, why not comics? Bill Morrison: "*The Simpsons* is a TV show in the world of *Futurama*, so what if Fry had a comic book of *The Simpsons* when he was a kid, and the brain spawn return and transport the Planet Express crew into the world of *The Simpsons*? And so I took that back to Matt [Groening] and pitched it. And he finally said, 'Ok you can do it.' "

As a huge fan of both shows, I am so grateful that Boothby and Morrison were so persistent on the idea to have these two worlds collide. The incredible issue was written by talented writer Ian Boothby. The award-winning comic book writer served as one of the lead writers for Bongo Comics, and this one in particular goes down as one of my all-time favorites among his works.

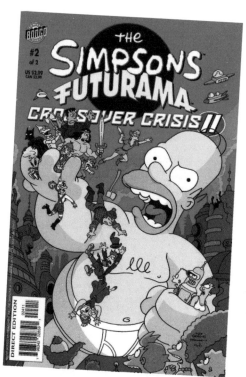

When I asked Boothby how he was able to cross over both shows' unique styles of humor, he said: "Humor in the *Futurama* world is darker than in *The Simpsons* because the 2000s were a darker time than the early '90s. But both shows are about family, one biological and one a work family, and looking at the world through a satirical perspective. It was fun playing with the similarities and differences."

This was followed up by a sequel in 2005, titled *The Simpsons Futurama Crossover Crisis II*.

I won't spoil the ending of these two crossover series, as I'd really recommend you read these for yourself. These were really fun limited series, and seeing the Simpsons interacting with the *Futurama* cast was surreal in the best way—and, in my humble opinion, more satisfying than the television crossover we got in 2014.

SIMPSONS COMICS PRESENTS

BART SIMPSON
★ MENACE TO SOCIETY ★

#5

US $2.50
CAN $3.50

DIRECT EDITION

SIMPSONS COMICS PRESENTS

BART SIMPSON
★ RABBLE ROUSER ★

#9

US $2.50
CAN $3.50

SIMPSONS COMICS PRESENTS

BART SIMPSON
★ TROUBLEMAKER ★

#3

US $2.50
CAN $3.50

DIRECT EDITION

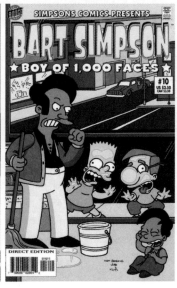

SIMPSONS COMICS PRESENTS

BART SIMPSON
BOY OF 1,000 FACES

#10

US $2.50
CAN $3.50

DIRECT EDITION

SIMPSONS COMICS PRESENTS

BART SIMPSON
★ JUVENILE JOKESTER ★

#4

US $2.50
CAN $3.50

SIMPSONS·COMICS·PRESENTS

BART SIMPSON
★ SON OF HOMER ★

#1

US $2.50
CAN $3.50

FANTABULOUS
1ST ISSUE
COLLECTOR'S
ITEM!

DIRECT EDITION

Bart Simpson Comics

Alongside the main series, Bongo also released *Simpsons Comics Present Bart Simpson*. The first issue was published in 2000 and ran for a hundred issues, until 2006. Whereas the *Simpsons Comics* focused on the family and supporting characters as a whole, these stories were focused squarely on America's favorite underachiever himself, Bart Simpson. These skewed toward a slightly younger audience than the main series. Ian Boothby says,

> "THE SIMPSONS [COMIC] WAS ALL AGES, I THINK THEY WANTED TO AIM A COMIC DIRECTLY AT KIDS. BART HAVING WILD ADVENTURES WITHOUT WORRYING WHAT HOMER AND MARGE THOUGHT OF THEM."

As we've explored in this book, El Barto has been featured front and center on most of the *Simpsons* merchandise, from T-shirts to video games. As one of the more recognizable and popular characters in the show, giving Bart his own solo comic title was only natural. The *Bart Simpson Comics* were also a callback to the comics that Bill Morrison grew up on, like *Richie Rich*, *Archie*, and *Dennis the Menace*. Morrison: "We wanted it to be all ages, so adult fans would enjoy it, but it would be an easy book for kids to get into as well. As we started to feature 'alternative' cartoonists in the title, like Evan Dorkin, Carol Lay, Peter Kuper, Sergio Aragonés, Scott Shaw, etc., it became my goal to make it the coolest kid book on earth. And it was for a while, until Chris Duffy did it better with *Spongebob Comics*."

The End of Bongo Comics

Bongo Comics closed its doors in October 2018. But within those successful twenty-five years, hundreds of stories, secrets, and reimaginations of the Simpsons family were shared with fans around the world. As a huge *Simpsons Comics* fan, I always felt part of another layer of the *Simpsons* fandom where we were privy to original stories that were never seen on screen. The voice of the comics toed the line of authenticity and complete originality. They built upon the characters and stories from the show, with the same quick and edgy humor that was present from the beginning, as well making the comics a standout amongst bookshelves and comic collections everywhere.

For me, I felt the passion the creators had for the comics imprinted on every page up until their very last issue…#245.

There is no definite answer as to why Bongo Comics ended. My personal theory is that comic sales, on the whole, had been in a steady decline for years. Similarly to newspaper, magazine, and even book publications, online content is so readily available now that many people choose to consume entertainment via tablets and phones. This movement, combined with the cost of writers, artists, and printers, may have been too much to keep *Simpsons Comics* going.

It is difficult to feel anything short of sadness when discussing "finality" in relation to *The Simpsons*. For many, myself included, the show is a soft, nostalgic, and warming part of our lives, where we are welcomed by the open arms of an eclectic group of lovable characters. The comics were a huge part of this comfortable escapism, opening up the world even wider, allowing us to get lost within the boundless corners of Springfield.

When I asked Ian Boothby about the legacy of *Simpsons Comics*, he said: "To a lot of people they were the first comic they read and how they were introduced to *The Simpsons*. Many times I've heard parents say that they wouldn't let their kids watch the show, but they were okay with them reading the comics. More than once I've been told the comics were how they learned to read."

Overall, *Simpsons Comics* was a massive collaboration between hundreds of writers, artists, and editors. It is obvious from reading these stories that these creatives really cared about their work, and that, just like us, they were huge fans of the show too.

Closing Thoughts

Out of any *Simpsons*-related merchandise covered in this book, I feel that *Simpsons Comics* above all deserves its own separate book. *Simpsons Comics* alone spans 245 issues, and that's not even mentioning the many offshoot comics, like *Bart Simpson*, *Itchy & Scratchy*, *Radioactive Man*, *One-Shot Wonders*, and *Treehouse of Horror*. I haven't even touched on the *Simpsons Comics One-Shot Wonders,* which were standalone issues specifically for individuals such as Ralph Wiggum, Milhouse, Professor Frink, Jimbo Jones–heck, even Duffman got his own comic! "Oh yeah!"

Writing this chapter has been a great excuse to go back and rediscover these comics that I loved as a child. *Simpsons Comics* were what I picked out to read on long drives with my family, it was what I sneaked into the shopping cart when my mum went to the grocery store, and it was what kept me up at night as I read the comic strips under my duvet with a flashlight. The TV show was not always accessible, but the comics always were.

CHAPTER SIX

Fast Food

WARREN EVANS

Here we arrive at something I'm sure all of us remember about the '90s: *fast food*…oh, and lots and lots of toys. We've talked all throughout this book about the absolute lack of pulling punches from the team when it came to general merchandise, with everything from a Bart Simpson tooth-brushing timer, all the way to a Homer cookie jar, and the same can be said for fast-food promotions.

What is it about this idea that feels so perfect? You mean to tell me that I can have a nice meal and have a toy to play with while I eat? *And* I can take it home? For as long as I can remember, a commercial about any sort of toy at the local McDonald's or Burger King would have me begging my mom to drive us down there for dinner, and there were plenty of Simpsons to go around.

Few things, even in my adult life, can match that feeling of looking at the fast-food menu and seeing which toys are available, taking note of which ones I have, and which one I really want. I'm sure my mom grew tired of me asking if there was a way to get more than one. Maybe part of the collecting bug started with many of us way back then?

Burger King

Throughout the '90s and well beyond, we saw the Simpsons team up with Burger King, Subway, KFC, Red Rooster, Church's, and more. I've always had a special place in my heart for this type of toy. I think some of the finest examples of this, when it comes to *The Simpsons*, are the infamous Burger King dolls and camping figures from back in 1990.

The camping set is another great example of how imperfect some of the earlier 3D renditions of the family are, but still with that charm I keep talking about. Each figure came with its own foldable background, so you could create a scene for your new toy. Many have cited "The Call of The Simpsons" from season one as the inspiration for this set, and I believe that has to be at least partially true. It's safe to assume that episode was in development while they searched for fun toy ideas. Also, like many toys from this time, the hollow body of the toys made them work perfectly as pencil toppers!

The BK dolls are particularly interesting because they seem to be based on the same sculpts that were also used in Japan by Avanti, as well as Jemini in France. At the very least, maybe they were handled by the same team. Either way, at $3.49 each, with the purchase of mini-muffins or any size fries of course, these dolls were a hit. They featured a soft plastic head, a plush body, a personalized tag shaped as an appropriate item—a skateboard for Bart, a saxophone for Lisa—and eyes that looked in different directions, almost as if they were looking to each other for the next move. The commercial for them also featured original animation, where Lisa and Bart argued over why anyone would want to play with them, followed by Homer screaming, *"Why would anyone play with any of you?"*

If you've ever been to a flea market or antique mall, you've seen at least three of the figures from one or both of these sets. I would even go so far as to say that at least 3 percent of eBay's revenue comes from the fees associated with selling these. (Not really, but who knows?) Either way, their commonness aside, these remain another wonderful glimpse into the beginning of the show. For a lot of people, these are probably some of the first, if not only, *Simpsons* toys they had!

Beyond that, when we look at any well-merchandised property over the last fifty years, having a large universe of characters will always help. *Star Wars* merchandise was able to do so much because they had a whole solar system to play with, and it seems like *The Simpsons* had a similar upside. Not only did we love the main characters, we also loved other versions of them, like those from Treehouse of Horror.

Burger King was known for tons of toys in this space, including Spooky Light-ups, Creepy Classics, and more. This seems to be some of the first merchandise, outside of the comics, to fully capitalize on the Halloween specials and really make it easy and fun to collect the characters from their favorite yearly tradition.

Spooky Light-ups would do exactly that: *light up!*…until the battery died, of course. Here we see plenty of familiar versions, like Marge as a witch and Grampa as a vampire, but also fun versions, like Lisa dressed as a ghost for Halloween, and Apu wearing a pumpkin costume. We even see Maggie dressed as a bat, with a pumpkin also decorated with a pacifier. These toys all had a built-in mechanism that would trigger a small light within part of the base. Ads would tell you to "collect all fifteen…if you dare!"

Creepy Classics also featured several characters you know, like "King Homer" and "Werewolf Flanders," but also Groundskeeper Willie as Gill-man from *The Creature from the Black Lagoon* and Marge as Franken-Marge, a parody of *Bride of Frankenstein*. Each toy came with a base that featured a pull tab that revealed the punchline via changing screen.

Around this time, Burger King made one of the most memorable fast-food products of the last thirty years: the class-disrupting, teacher-maddening, parent-frustrating, talking watches:

Who wouldn't want a watch with the Simpsons on it? This is a space the show utilized with other promotions, as well as in general merchandise, but these BK watches broke new ground. You had snowboarding Bart, Krusty speaking to the audience, Homer grilling up some burgers—in fact, his watch literally said "Mmm…burger"—as well as the entire family in the car. "Are we there yet? Are we there yet?" If you ever had one of these, I don't think it's possible not to have at least one story where you had to leave it with the principal. Truly a watch fit for Bart.

CHAPTER SIX: FAST FOOD

When it comes to collecting anything, the more obscure always grabs me. Collections like this give you more of Springfield. This falls right in with a growing desire for that among collectors, as we saw in other chapters. Where the team might have been unsure about an Otto or Skinner toy in the beginning, by 2000, there was no doubt. Not so sure? Well, let's look at another line of BK figures that were released to celebrate the *Global Fan Fest*—a yearlong celebration honoring the tenth anniversary of the show, as well as receiving a star on the Hollywood Walk of Fame.

But what about *The Simpsons* Movie? I'm sure we all remember how excited we were when this was first announced. The movie is now old enough to see itself. In addition to that, these toys could talk! Whether it was Lisa saying, "We have to save Springfield!" or Chief Wiggum saying, "Stop in the name of squeamishness!" each had a button that would fire off a catchphrase. All fifteen figures also had a "solid gold" version, but the catchphrase remained the same.

Ads for the BK Movie toys are also a nice reminder that by 2007, a lot of people had grown up significantly with the show. One ad shows the parents playing loudly with the toys at the table, while the kids get annoyed and take them away. To me this was a super fun way to remind people the show is for all of us!

While the movie had other toys made by companies like McFarlane (as seen in chapter one), these small toys seem to be the main things many of us remember. While my brain wants to understand why they didn't make a *lot* more movie-centric toys, I tend to explain it away by realizing they wore the same clothes. Makes sense, right?

Burger King continued to work with the show for a while, but one of my favorite sets came only a year later, in 2008, with this connectable set of couch figures. Each piece worked on its own, but when connected, one piece could trigger the entire couch. This is an idea and mechanism almost too good for fast food, because you instantly feel like you need the entire couch! Marge's hair would spin, Lisa would move from side to side with her sax, Bart would raise his arm with remote in hand, Homer would raise his arms in a very "Woo-hoo!" fashion, while Maggie popped out from underneath a couch cushion. Hard to beat that.

KFC

However, none of that stopped them from teaming up with other fast-food giants. Sliding back a few years, KFC not only ran great ad campaigns, like Homer sneaking out via an underground tunnel to grab some chicken, or hiding from the cops after receiving a free two-liter of 7 Up, but also made some of my favorite fast-food products:

These cup toppers would stand out in any collection, and this trend is almost worthy of being called a "lost art." Everything from *Star Wars* to *Shrek* had cup toppers, but as usual, nobody did it quite like *The Simpsons*. The only downside is that we didn't get a Maggie. Don't ask me why. (Oh, and yes, their arms move.)

Subway

Subway even got in on the action, with a line of toys that each had their own gimmick. Bart with his wind-up skateboard, Homer with a pull string drawing him closer to his tray of donuts, Lisa and her saxophone acting as a whistle, and Bartman acting almost as a fidget spinner—these could entertain any kid (or adult) for quite a while.

International

International markets like Red Rooster and Hungry Jacks also made toys, but collectors in the US had to spend just a little more time tracking those down. I've heard stories of people making connections across the globe, just to trade their regional *Simpsons* gear. This is one of the things that makes me love this hobby as much as I do, and for this long…this sense of collaboration over competition. Here are a few of those toys…

Much like the BK couch I mentioned earlier, a few years before that, Hungry Jacks—the Australian equivalent to Burger King—released sets like this beach scene and surfboard set. To me, items like the beach scene are even more brilliant than a set of individual figures, because this is almost a puzzle, and no one likes missing pieces! But unlike what came after, these didn't have a gimmick outside of fitting together.

I think fast-food toys in general make a great metaphor for the entire hobby. The sense of completion exists, but also the sense of memory, the sense of nostalgia. Some of us probably remember trying our best to have all five dolls, or every Creepy Classic, while others probably remember the Camping Lisa as their favorite toy to play with in the car on the way to Grandma's house.

For my part in this book, I've tried to share the sheer volume of product in as broad a way as possible, but I also find myself wanting to explain that collecting is what you want it to be. There is no right or wrong way to collect. A small collection that means a lot to you is just as valuable as the rarest collection in the world. All five BK dolls from 1990 might mean as much to you for the memories as anything on this earth, and that's an idea I really like.

Doritos*

*

Sonic Sour Cream
FLAVOUR
SAVEUR DE
Crème Sure Sonique

PEEL TO WIN · COLLECTIBLE STICKER
4 OF 5 BAGS CONTAIN STICKER. DETAILS ON BACK.

FREE
The SIMPSONS™
GRATUIT

DÉCOLLEZ POUR GAGNER · AUTOCOLLANT. DÉTAILS AU VERSO.
4 SACS SUR 5 CONTIENNENT UN AUTOCOLLANT.

MATT GROENING

85 g
CHIPS TORTILLA CHIPS

CHAPTER SEVEN

Food & Drinks

JAMES HICKS

Who among us *hasn't* begged a parent to buy us a candy bar, or cereal, for the sole reason that it had a character we liked printed on the packaging? It didn't matter if the cereal tasted like literal cardboard, or if the chocolate tasted like crud; if it was endorsed by our favorite cartoon, we wanted it!

The Simpsons knew this better than anyone. As you have seen throughout this book, stick that yellow family on absolutely anything, and we suckers were more than willing to shell out a few extra bucks.

If you think of any food item, there's a high chance "*The Simpsons* did it!" From Jelly lollipops to macaroni and cheese. From breath mints to ice cream. Chocolate, cereal, cheese, donuts, soda, you name it, they appeared on it. Who is Homer Simpson to turn down food?

As with any *Simpsons*-related product, there are collectors who specifically search for these food-related tie-ins. This is perhaps a more challenging collecting niche because of the rarity and cost of the items—all because it's perishable. Plastic *Simpsons* action figures were made to be durable and last, but food was made to be consumed, and the packaging discarded.

So, whereas some collectors use the rarity of food merchandise as a motivator, others are deterred. There is also the fact that the contents can leak, smell, and spoil as all foods do eventually. As such, many collectors have wisely chosen to throw away the perishables entirely, purely preserving the packaging for display.

In this chapter we'll be going over the delicious, and sometimes not so edible, world of Simpsons food and beverage tie-ins. So bon appétit!

Butterfinger

Although you may find it hard to believe, some people's first introduction to *The Simpsons* wasn't through the television show, but rather, Butterfinger! The Simpsons were the official mascot for the crunchy peanut butter chocolate on and off since the early Tracy Ullman days, and the brand's catchphrase, "Nobody better lay a finger on my Butterfinger," was said by kids in playgrounds everywhere in the early '90s. And despite never being said in the show, it also became one of Bart Simpson's signature catchphrases.

The very first Simpsons Butterfinger commercial was shown on TV in 1988, a year before the Simpsons starred in their very own prime-time show. This commercial also marked the first appearance of Bart's blue-haired sidekick, Milhouse, who did not appear in the shorts. Designed purely for this commercial, the "dud" didn't debut in the show until a year later, in "Simpsons Roasting on an Open Fire."

Although this may be sacrilegious to say, the Butterfinger commercials were better animated than most of the Tracy Ullman shorts. The movements felt more fluid, and there was more detail in the background characters and settings. This was because the shorts were produced on a shoestring budget with a short turnaround, whereas the Butterfinger commercials had more money put into their production.

Bart Simpson quickly became Butterfinger's mascot and was featured heavily in their promotions and commercials throughout the late '80s, '90s and early 2000s. The cross-promotion was a huge success for both Nestle and FOX. Butterfinger bars introduced the relatively unknown Simpsons family to millions of people back when they were only shorts in a comedy sketch show. And when the Simpsons went on to star in their own television series and become a ratings hit and cultural phenomenon, the Butterfinger brand benefited massively.

The Butterfinger marketing department had a lot of fun with the *Simpsons* brand, taking advantage of the show's growing success and quirky characters. In 1991, you could find horoscopes inside the wrappers with Bart in assorted Zodiac illustrations, and they also did several *Simpsons*-related competitions and giveaways over the years.

They gave away a copy of *Simpsons Illustrated* in one promotion, with other prizes including *Simpsons* wristwatches as well as gold, silver, and bronze medals—embossed with Bart.

The long-running Butterfinger and *Simpsons* collaboration came to an end in 2001. Why Nestle chose to terminate their partnership is unclear, maybe *The Simpsons's* creators no longer saw as much value in the collaboration as they once did? Maybe Butterfinger felt they had reaped enough success from the show's catapult to fame? No matter the answer, what is clear is that FOX now had no obligations to the peanut butter brand, meaning that *The Simpsons* now had free rein to take swipes at its old nutty friend. In season thirteen's "Sweet and Sour Marge," released around the end of their partnership, the town decides to outlaw sugar. So, the townsfolk are forced to watch the police burn their beloved chocolate. But when they toss an armful of Butterfingers into the fire, they don't burn, with Chief Wiggum summing up, "Even the fire doesn't want them." Interestingly, in the DVD commentary for the episode, Al Jean said this about the Butterfinger contract: "If it had still been in existence, we wouldn't have done it."

Despite this jab at their product, twelve years later, Nestle reunited with the Bartman, launching a nationwide sweepstakes entitled, "Who Stole Bart's Butterfinger?"

In 2012, fans were called on to help solve "the crispety, crunchety crime of the century" by finding codes inside the wrappers and entering them on Butterfinger's website. If you were successful, you could win one of 100,000 instant prizes, including Homer Simpson snowboards, Bart Simpson cruzers (from Santa Cruz Skateboards), *Simpsons* Kidrobot figurines, and a digital download of the *Simpsons* episode "Treehouse of Horror II." The grand prize included a trip to Los Angeles and a personalized illustrated portrait in the *Simpsons* style.

So, who did steal Bart's Butterfinger? Well, out of twelve potential suspects, it was... Milhouse! A very fitting end to the sweepstake seeing as his character first debuted in the Butterfinger commercials.

This competition was ultimately the final time Butterfinger and *The Simpsons* teamed up and although Bart has not been their official mascot for over a decade now, we still can't help but think of *The Simpsons* whenever we see a Butterfinger bar.

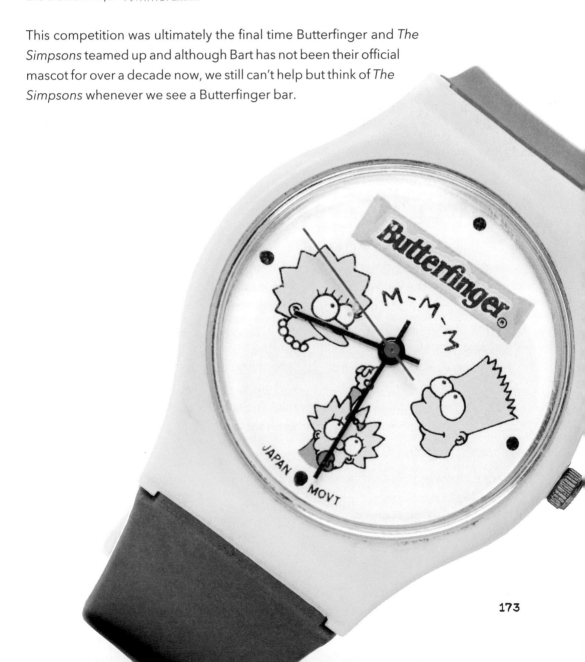

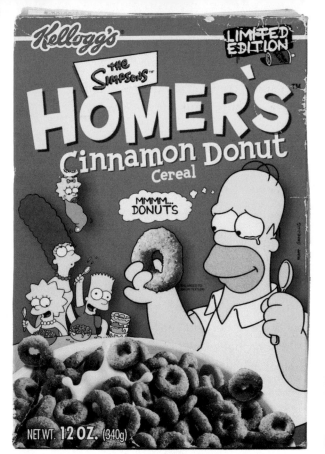

Kellogg's Cereal

In 2001, in a partnership with Kellogg's, *The Simpsons* released two limited-edition cereals. The first was Homer's Cinnamon Donut, and the second Bart Simpson's Peanut Butter Crunch. The packaging for both of these cereals is fantastic. The back of the Homer's Cinnamon Donut box even has a page from the show's fictional *The Springfield Shopper* newspaper with articles about the town. The headline "Springfield Power Plant Now Safer Than Ever" appears at the top, and the article talks about the "new record of fourteen straight accident-free days shattering the plant's old record of ten days." Other articles include "Principal Skinner Changes Home Phone Number Again," which details Seymour's "malicious phone prank." The article goes on to say that "Mr. Skinner is confident that his new private, unlisted phone number will end the nightly torment," before giving away the new number.

There's also a word search where you circle characters' names, as well as a word scramble. At the bottom right-hand side is the classified ads section, which lists a garage sale that is literally giving away a garage. This attention to detail only personalized the product more, making a child's morning that much more fun by allowing them to

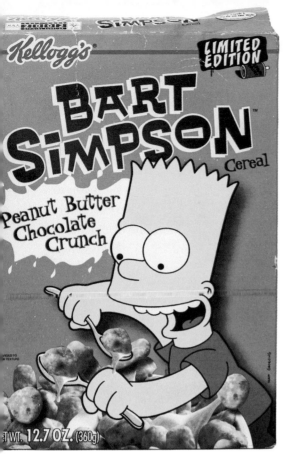

experience *The Simpsons* away from the TV…as well as distracting from any slow sense of impending doom in anticipation of another day at school.

Both of these cereals were essentially promotions for the newly released *Simpsons Road Rage* video game, with the sides of the cereal boxes offering ten dollars off the video game using the promotion code inside.

As for the taste? Well, the only reviews online are of people eating twenty-years-out-of-date stale cereal, so they're not the most reliable taste tests. But Homer's Cinnamon Donuts was said to have an intense, almost overwhelming cinnamon flavor—which probably explains why it wasn't around for too long!

Kellogg's worked with *The Simpsons* again in 2002 and 2003 to release Bart Simpson's No ProblemOs and Bart Simpson's Eat My Shorts cereal. They were released only in the United Kingdom and Australia.

While these particular four Kellogg's cereals were all original, the next cereal *The Simpsons* brought out was ripped straight out of the show…

Krusty-O's Cereal

Krusty-O's, a formally fictional cereal that first appeared in the 1995 episode " 'Round Springfield," actually became a real product in 2007!

To promote the newly released *Simpsons Movie*, FOX partnered with 7-Eleven to retrofit select convenience stores, across the country, into Kwik-E-Marts. So customers could now buy real-life products that they saw in the animated series, one of which was Frosted Krusty-O's. This was an incredibly clever piece of advertising that is known as "reverse product placement," where a company creates real products to match those seen in a fictional setting, essentially bringing a fake item into the real world.

But the fictional item didn't have the best reputation in the show. In " 'Round Springfield," Bart accidentally eats the free jagged metal prize included in his cereal. The sharp, tiny object becomes lodged inside him, causing Bart to require surgery. When Krusty is held accountable for this, he tries to prove to the press that the jagged metal piece is harmless by eating it, but instead he swallows a *regular* Krusty-O, which in itself is so bad, that eating a single piece causes Krusty to double over in pain: "This thing is shredding my insides!"

But do not worry, Krusty did learn his lesson and recalled the jagged metal prize, replacing it with a coveted "flesh-eating bacteria" prize instead.

So, Krusty-O's, with the rep it had, was an odd food item to market to real customers, especially as the real box they released has Krusty on the cover holding a bowl of cereal loops, worms, mold, nails, and yes, a jagged metal piece. Thankfully, this is probably the first time in history that customers were happy that the product looked nothing like the packaging, because the cereal instead looked, tasted, and smelled like Froot Loops. This is because Krusty-O's were, in fact, Tootie Fruities cereal made by the Malt-O-Meal corporation, who simply rebranded the cereal for *The Simpsons Movie* promotion.

This *Simpsons* and 7-Eleven promotion was a huge success, with hundreds of fans crossing state lines just to visit these "Kwik-E-Marts." In July 2007, ABC News reported, "Fans of the hit TV show seem to be jumping at the chance to buy the other once-fictional products. The number of customers walking through the doors at these special stores has roughly doubled, as have sales, according to the company."

It's unfortunate that Krusty-O's were only a short-lived promotional tie-in, even if they were only rebranded Tootie Fruities. At Universal Studios, the Kwik-E-Mart gift shop has displays of false Krusty-O's boxes as the facade, so it could be a great opportunity to sell them there. But cereal-sellers may be upset, as the original four-dollar boxes now sell for up to forty dollars online!

Donuts

Who has seen a glistening pink sprinkled donut without *The Simpsons* instantly springing to mind? The dessert has become so synonymous with the brand that it was featured heavily in most advertising materials for *The Simpsons Movie*, with every trailer and poster using that half-eaten doughy pink icon for the letter O. In fact, the iconography of the donut is so tied to *The Simpsons* that it serves as a secondary logo for the show, appearing on T-shirts, plushies, magnets, and more.

So it should come as no surprise that its main consumer and ambassador, Homer Simpson, has appeared in many real-life donut promotions over the years, most famously with Krispy Kreme—a match made in advertising heaven!

But still, these promotions were only tying in with existing brands, just featuring the Simpsons on the packaging—whereas, when I was younger, I always dreamt of trying the "real" cartoon donut, and was perpetually disappointed that donuts in real life never looked half as good as the animated ones. So imagine my excitement when I discovered that you could finally buy a Lard Lad Donut for real in 2013. Based on the fictional donut shop from the show, Universal Studios parks have been selling the Big Pink Donut for close to a decade now.

These donuts are huge! Coming in at a whopping eight inches in diameter and weighing fourteen ounces, they are roughly the size of a large adult hand (or a child's head). Lard Lad also makes a variety of other flavors, including pink sweet creamy frosting and sprinkles, Chocolate Glazed, Maple Bacon, S'mores, and Oreo.

Lard Lad Donuts bakers start work at one o'clock every morning, to make fresh, soft donuts on-site. The center holes are cut by hand, and they are packaged in individual white boxes, encasing the freshness. The final touch is the Lard Lad sticker placed on the clear plastic window—they make for fantastic pictures.

Now, if you'll excuse me, I'm currently salivating over my keyboard.

Duff Beer

In 2016, Duff Beer made it onto *Time's* "Most Influential Fake Companies of All Time" list, being above Bubba Gump Shrimp, Good Burger, and the Krusty Krab. This makes sense, as the Duff brand has been a part of pop culture since 1990, first appearing in the third episode, *Homer's Odyssey*.

> **"DUFF! THE BEER THAT MAKES THE DAYS FLY BY! GIMME THAT WONDERFUL DUFF!"**

The fictional beverage was inspired by the Budweiser brand, sharing a similar red label, as well as Spandex-clad, cape-wearing superhero mascots, Budman and Duffman. Not a very subtle homage, but then again, this is *The Simpsons*.

Duff has appeared in the show perhaps more than most regular characters. Not only is it Homer's drink of choice at Moe's, but who could forget the part it played in creating "Lisa the Lizard Queen"? This is when Lisa drank a brown liquid, that we can only assume is Duff, during the Little Land of Duff ride, all accompanied by the "dulcet tones" of *The Simpsons*'s "It's a Small World" parody:

> **"DUFF BEER FOR ME,**
> **DUFF BEER FOR YOU,**
> **I'LL HAVE A DUFF,**
> **YOU'LL HAVE ONE TOO..."**

Given the recognizable brand marketability that Duff had around the world, it seemed like a foregone conclusion that the fictional beer would become a reality. But, surprisingly, officially licensed Duff is a relatively new product. I say "officially" because many bootleg Duff brands have been on shop shelves for decades.

In fact, Matt Groening never wanted to brew Duff licensed beer, over concerns that it would encourage children to drink. So with no official Duff Beer being sold, many entrepreneurs saw a lucrative gap in the market. As with the case of bootleg *Simpsons* T-shirts, people began counterfeiting their own Duffs with the intention of capitalizing on the inbuilt brand recognition. As a result, FOX and their blue-haired lawyers have been fighting against imitation Duffs for decades across the world, from Australia to Chile.

After years of legal action, and thousands of liters of knock-off Duff down the drain, FOX finally concluded, if you can't beat them, join them. In 2015, Jeffrey Godsick, president of the media company's consumer products division, told the *Wall Street Journal*, "Once you see enough piracy, you are faced with two choices. One is deciding to fight it, and the other is deciding to go out [into the market] with it."

With that, FOX brought on a British brewer, Paul Farnsworth, to create the recipe for an officially licensed Duff. After the developing stage, Jeffrey Godsick described the taste of the official Duff as having hints of fruit and caramel. "It's got a very good balance of flavor and refreshment to it. It's fairly deep golden in color. It's got a hint of fruit to it. It's got a caramel aroma to it."

The intention was to combat brandjacking of their IP by selling the real thing to consumers directly. That way FOX could control the quality of it themselves, so inferior products couldn't potentially damage their brand—not to mention the financial benefits!

Universal Studios have been selling Duff in their California and Florida parks since 2013. These were the first, and are still currently the only, two places in the United States where you can enjoy an officially licensed Duff Beer, with the beverage still yet to be sold publicly in US stores. It is sold in their expanded Springfield in Moe's Tavern and the Duff Brewery. It is available in Duff, Duff Lite, and Duff Dry, but as everyone knows who's seen the season four episode "Duffless," they all come from the same pipe anyway! For an extra fee, you can purchase a souvenir plastic pilsner with a Duff logo printed on it.

The person who helped bring Universal Studios' Duff to life was Executive Chef Steven Jayson, the man behind the famous Butter Beer. After experimenting with a dozen versions of the iconic drink, Jayson flew to California for a taste test with creators Matt Groening and James L. Brooks.

Although Matt Groening did not approve of selling Duff Beer, prior to its production in 2013, FOX had no issue with selling Duff energy drinks from as early as 2008. Under license from FOX, Boston America Corp. manufactured Duff energy drinks that looked identical to the Duff cans from the animated series. However, selling a nonalcoholic drink in packaging identical to the original alcoholic beverage was bound to cause some controversy. And, as Groening predicted, some parents were concerned that it would encourage children to drink, akin to selling candy cigarettes.

It does appear that the Duff energy drinks are now discontinued, with prices going as high as fifteen dollars for a single unopened can on eBay. Although the energy drinks may be gone, Boston America Corp. continues to sell Duff A L'Orange Soda, essentially just dropping the caffeine from its ingredients. If you're wanting to try a can, the soda is available to buy at Universal Studios, or more specifically, Apu's Kwik-E-Mart.

Duff

A L'ORANGE
SPARKLING BEVERAGE

12 FL OZ (355mL)

Squishee

In addition to stocking KrustyOs during the 7-Eleven promotion with *The Simpsons Movie*, you could have also purchased a Squishee in special collector cups. This was a cross-promotion made in heaven, seeing as the fictional Squishee is an obvious parody of the Slurpee sold by 7-Eleven. The frozen syrup drink first appeared in season one's fifth episode, *Bart the General*, when Nelson's minions discussed what kind of Squishee they brought, with "blue" apparently being a flavor.

For many of us who grew up with *The Simpsons*, the Squishee has become so entwined with our association with ice slush drinks, I find myself subconsciously asking for a Squishee rather than a Slurpee in stores, cinemas, and yes, 7-Elevens.

Although the 7-Eleven Squishees were just rebranded Slurpees, you can buy official Squishees in Universal Studios Hollywood and Orlando (as well as souvenir green Squishee cups), and a real-life Kwik-E-Mart store in Myrtle Beach, South Carolina.

These Squishees are sold in a variety of flavors: White Cherry, Raspberry Lemonade, and Banana, although we *Simpsons* fans won't be satisfied until every Squishee flavor from the show becomes available, from chutney and wheatgrass to high-protein beef. And unfortunately, these places will probably never offer an "all-syrup super Squishee" that'll cause you to go on a sugar-crazed rampage around town, like Bart and Milhouse in "Boy-Scoutz 'n The Hood."

Flaming Moe

Aside from the Squishees and Duff Beers, the signature beverage sold at Universal Studios is the Flaming Moe. A real-life recreation of the iconic drink from the episode, well…"Flaming Moe's." In this season three classic, Homer needed a drink to get through his sisters-in-law's boring slideshow of their holiday. But with Patty swiping his last Duff, Homer had to improvise. So, grabbing every alcoholic bottle he could find in his cupboards, he poured every last drop into his blender. Adding a few dashes of Krusty's Non-Narkotik Kough Syrup, he mixed the concoction together. It passed the first test: it didn't cause Homer to go blind, which was a great start! But what really improved the flavor was Patty's cigarette ashes. which set his drink aflame. "I didn't know the scientific explanation, but fire made it good!"

And so the Flaming Homer was born! At least, it was until Moe took credit for it and rebranded the drink, and his tavern, to the Flaming Moe.

So when Universal Studios opened the *Simpsons*-themed areas in California and Florida, people could now visit Moe's Tavern in real life and enjoy a steaming cup of Flaming Moe.

But, as Homer's random collection of ingredients would have violated several health laws, the beverage sold at Universal Studios is simply a nonalcoholic orange soda served over dry ice. Despite looking nothing like the original purple drink from the show, the real appeal of this beverage is the smoke effect, as well as the souvenir cup, which has flames printed on it along with the Flaming Moe logo. The bottom part of the container holds the dry ice, which escapes through small holes and bubbles up toward the surface, giving it a flame-like effect. The plastic cup is detachable and reusable.

Flaming Moe is also available as an energy drink, which can be found online and in a few select stores. This officially licensed drink is made by Boston America Corp., the company behind the Duff soda cans.

Allen's *Simpsons* Soft Drinks

The earliest known *Simpsons* soft drinks were made by the brand Allen's in 1991, and were sold in Canada. Each flavor's can had different art printed on it; Wild Apple Berry had Bart on a skateboard with a speech bubble containing his signature catchphrase, "Cowabunga!"

Grape Cocktail had the masked Bartman saying, "Watch it, dude!"

Apple Cherry had Bart on a skateboard again, but this time saying, "Yo!"

These cans are very rare and difficult to find online. Allen's also released *Simpsons* drinks in juice boxes. As of the time of writing, there was a single empty carton of Bart Simpson Wild Apple Cherry being sold for $17.77 on eBay.

Hall & Woodhouse *Simpsons* Soda

British brewery Hall & Woodhouse released a line of *Simpsons* cans exclusively in the United Kingdom in 1999. The designs for these are more fun than a soda can ought to be. For example, Homer's D'oh Bad Apple Crush Flavor has Homer literally being crushed by a giant apple. Around the rim is a sinister-looking Mr. Burns with text that reads, "Radioactive mutant apple does not exist…a spokesman for Mr. Burns stated today."

The grape and cherry flavor is called Blues and features two jazz-playing Lisas. The text at the bottom reads "100% pure" with the text "depression" crossed out, and "soul" underneath it.

Cherry Bomb has an image of Bart dunking a "Krusty bomb."

A Hall & Woodhouse soda not featured in the images was Krusty's Yellow Kola that is "90 percent safe!" It also features the highly dubious claim that "nine out of ten children can't tell the difference." This particular can is the most expensive, with one listed on eBay for almost forty dollars.

CHAPTER EIGHT

Board Games

JAMES HICKS

The very second episode of *The Simpsons*, "Bart the Genius," opens with the family playing a game of Scrabble, and if viewers had missed the first episode when it aired, this scene would've perfectly caught them up on the family's personalities and quirks.

Father, Homer, plays "do," instead of "oxidize," despite the word already laid out for him. Daughter, Lisa, gets a triple word score by playing the word "id"…which Homer questions and refers to the family dictionary (conveniently propping up the short leg of the couch). Bart, the son, then plays "Kwyjibo," defining it as "A big, dumb, balding, North American ape with no chin," a.k.a. Homer—sending the dad into an uncontrollable rage which mother Marge fails to calm down, instead resorting to salvaging the explosion of letter tiles that Homer sends flying as he flips the table.

This two-minute opening, set around a seemingly ordinary game of Scrabble, showed audiences that this family could be just like us. A lower-income middle-class family with wonky furniture legs, a short-tempered husband, a patient wife, an intelligent daughter, and a rebellious, cheeky son.

I'm sure that, when the creators made this episode, they had no idea that fifteen years later, Scrabble would release a real-life *Simpsons* version of the classic game that families just like the Simpsons would play together. This was a version complete with yellow tiles, a board that featured up to a hundred of their characters, and its own rules too, with words such as Bart's "Kwyjibo" being an acceptable word…which we are sure has caused *many* disgruntled fathers to flip a table.

However, *The Simpsons*'s history with board games goes back much further than the Scrabble edition, with the family getting some of their own board games back in 1990, including *The Simpsons* Mystery of Life by Cardinal Industries, and Milton Bradley's Don't Have a Cow Dice Game.

The former challenges players to pull "the scariest face," or belch the "biggest burp" to win donuts. This is very in keeping with the TV show's humor, as we look back on Bart's funny faces in the family's portraits and Barney's incessant burping.

These board games were followed by 1991's The *Simpsons* Board Game by Paul Lamond Games. One detail I do have to mention about this game is the fake dollar bills that feature Springfield's town founder, and certainly *not* a pirate, Jebediah Springfield. The thick black borders and penciling make the design feel it's been ripped straight out of the television show.

I adore the '90s feel of these particular board games. As was typical of the very early '90s *Simpsons* merchandise, the pink and green color scheme is a running theme and one I genuinely wish they would bring back. The box art, board itself, and character tokens are drawn with that endearing early janky style. And, although the animation in *The Simpsons* today is certainly flawless, I can't help but miss the early hand-drawn roughness that made it so charming to begin with.

I personally feel that, as the years go by for *Simpsons* merchandising in general, the style becomes far too templated. There just aren't any imperfections, which were so fitting for what I would consider TV's "imperfect family." Every piece of merchandise now is exactly on model, which I understand is perhaps a strange thing to complain about.

We can see this change distinctly when we flash forward twenty years, to the 2000 version of The *Simpsons* Board Game, this time made by Winning Moves. Just comparing this box to the 1991 version, we can see this drastic style change, which is to be expected after two decades. But I can't help but feel that the art style of the 2000 The *Simpsons* Board Game just looks so unoriginal and bland compared to the '90s version—but this all comes down to personal taste, of course. I realize I'm starting to look like an old man yelling at a cloud.

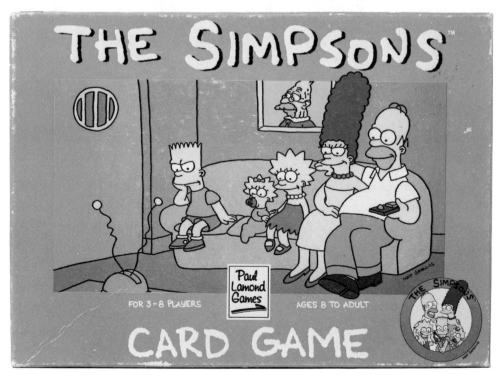

It's not only the boxes that are different, because despite sharing the same name, the two versions of The *Simpsons* Board Game differ drastically in gameplay. The 2000 edition has you playing as a Simpson family member, collecting tokens that are significant to that character. There's Duff Beer for Homer, or a dummy for Maggie, with the object of the game being to litter the carpet with your tokens. There is one central game board and six sub-games, with the most fun being "Principal Skinner's IQ Test," which has you answer *Simpsons* trivia questions. These range from the relatively easy for casual fans, to some that will have even the most knowledgeable fans scratching their heads. One in particular is:

> "IN 'SUNDAY, CRUDDY SUNDAY,' WHAT MAGAZINE IS SEEN IN
> THE TIRE SHOP WAITING ROOM?
>
> A. BUNGO TODAY
> B. CYCLE FREAKS
> C. BURN RUBBER
> D. TROUT FEVER"

Most fans are probably unaware of these original *Simpsons* games and are far more familiar with the major licensed ones. From Monopoly to Jeopardy, and checkers to chess, if a board game exists, then it's highly likely that there's a *Simpsons* version of it. I don't know why, but playing a tired old game with a *Simpsons* makeover just makes the experience more fun. If you were to ask me to sit down and play Monopoly for the next four hours, I wouldn't be interested, but if you presented me with the *Simpsons* version, then I'd be there, ready to buy up every Springfield property and become richer than the Rich Texan—yee-haw!

Speaking of Monopoly, the season thirteen episode, "Brawl in the Family," perfectly encapsulates what it's like to play this board game with your family. It starts with picking one of the many different versions, whether it's "Star Wars Monopoly, Rasta-Monopoly, Gallup-oligopoly, or Edna Krabappoly." Then, after a few hours of playing, the game ultimately ends with Bart cheating and the family strangling each other, leading to the police having to come around to break up yet "another case of Monopoly-related violence."

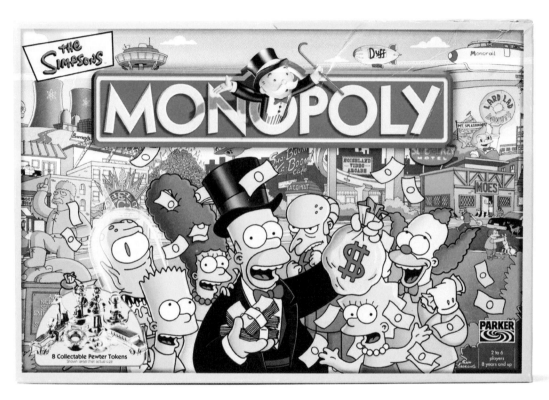

Only one year before the release of this episode in 2001, Hasbro had released the *Simpsons* Monopoly edition. But unlike the original game, where you had to choose to play as a thimble, top hat, or iron…

MARGE: "HOW CAN AN IRON BE A LANDLORD?"

…the *Simpsons* version has tokens such as: Blinky, a Jebediah Springfield statue, Santa's Little Helper, Kang, Homer as the Monorail Conductor, and Bart in a Soap Box Racer—although other versions include a donut and a school bus. In addition to these, extra mail-in tokens were available to order, like Lisa, Marge holding Maggie, Otto, and Mr. Burns. As these did not come with the box, they are a lot rarer and more expensive, with this token set recently selling on eBay for over $400!

The Simpsons Monopoly maintained the show's color scheme with yellow dice and yellow and blue houses. The money also had different characters on it, with Maggie on the 1, Lisa on the 5, Bart on the 10, Homer on the 20, Marge on the 50, Grandpa on the 100, and the 500-note of course featuring the wealthiest of Springfieldians, Mr. Burns.

One nice detail I particularly liked was the "go to jail free" chance card, featuring Chief Wiggum dragging Snake Jailbird to jail.

The town of Springfield lends itself well to the Monopoly board, featuring iconic locations from the show. Springfield is a character unto itself, and the businesses are just as iconic as its characters, with the Kwik-E-Mart, Android's Dungeon and Baseball Card Shop, and Moe's all being properties you can buy. There are also other iconic locations from the show, including Duff Gardens (the site where Lisa the Lizard Queen hallucinated after drinking the black liquid), Itchy and Scratchy Land (where the Simpsons took down killer robots), and The Happy Sumo (where Homer ate a poisonous fugu and thought he was going to die).

But there is not just one, but three different *Simpsons* Monopoly games. In 2005, Hasbro brought out the Treehouse of Horror Collector's Edition, as wellas an electronic banking edition in 2007.

While *The Simpsons* Monopoly is probably the most well-known, there were plenty more *Simpsons* editions of board games brought out around the early 2000s.

BART SIMPSON™
KARTENSPIEL
THE SIMPSONS™
MATT GROENING
NA WARTE! DU....
MATT GROENING
TM& © 1991 Twentieth Century Fox Film Corporation.
All Rights Reserved. Licensed by MERCHANDISING MÜNCHEN KG
ASS
Altenburg Stralsunder

BART SIMPSON™
KARTENSPIEL

Wer beim BART SIMPSON Kartenspiel an sich denkt, hat an alle gedacht. In diesem Spiel ist Vorsicht besser als Nachsicht. 'Ne echt trübe Tasse hat keinen Durchblick!

mein Spiel

In the 2003 episode, "'Tis the Fifteenth Season," Bart is given a Krusty Brand Operation Game for Christmas which includes such child-friendly phases as, "Oh, you just tweezered my wang!"

In the very same year this episode was released, Hasbro released an official *Simpsons* Operation game. But instead of having Krusty the Clown as the patient, Homer took to the doctor's table. This does actually make sense, seeing as Homer has had many operations over the course of thirty years, from his triple bypass surgery to breaking every bone in his body falling down Springfield Gorge.

The game plays the same as the standard *Operation*: if your tweezers brush the metal while extracting his bones, pretzels, or hammer? Then Homer yelps out a few phases such as, "D'oh!" "Yikes!" and strangely, "Wahoo," for some reason.

HOMER'S GOT PROBLEMS: A PEA BRAIN, THUMB, AND MORE. IN THIS CLASSIC GAME YOU GET TO BE HIS SURGEON. CAN YOU SETTING OFF THE BUZZER — AND HOMER'S B

IF YOU TOUCH THE SIDES WITH THE TWEEZE GROAN, OR GIVE YOU A PIECE OF HIS MIN ONE). EARN MONEY BY PERFORMING SUCCE NICE, QUIET KIND, WITH NO BUZZERS OR B SAID AND DONE, THE RICHEST DOCTOR WINS!

The HASBRO, MILTON BRADLEY and MB names and logos are ® and © All Rights Reserved. TM and ® denote U.S. Trademarks. Color and part MADE IN U.S.A. WITH TWEEZERS, LIGHT BULB AND MODULE MADE IN C

Manufacturer's representative in the United Kingdom is Hasbro UK Ltd. 4YH. Tel: 00800 22427276. Distributed in Australia by Hasbro Australi NSW 2122, Australia. Tel: (02) 9874-0999. Distributed in New Zealand 100-940, North Shore Mail Centre, Auckland, New Zealand. Tel: (09) 9 address for future reference. Hasbro Canada, Longueuil, QC Canada J4

THE SIMPSONS TM & © 2005. Twentieth Century Fox Film Corporation

OPERATION is a registered trademark, licensed for use by Hasbro, Inc.

Closing Thoughts

I have taken this chapter to discuss only a select few of the many licensed Simpsonized board games. But there are other, countless, ones to find: Uno, Guess Who, Clue, and Wheel of Fortune—and that's not even mentioning *The Simpsons* puzzles, which I've counted at least forty of during my research.

Growing up, I remember that many of my friends, even those who didn't watch the show, had at least one *Simpsons* licensed board game in their cupboard. In fact, I'm sure there are many of you reading this right now who grew up only playing the Simpsonized version of a particular board game, and may never have even played the classic version.

Writing this chapter has been a great excuse for me to pull out and dust off my collection of *Simpsons* board games to play with my friends and family—even if it did result in a few who stubbornly refused to accept "Kwyjibo" as a triple word score.

THIS PATIENT TALKS BACK!

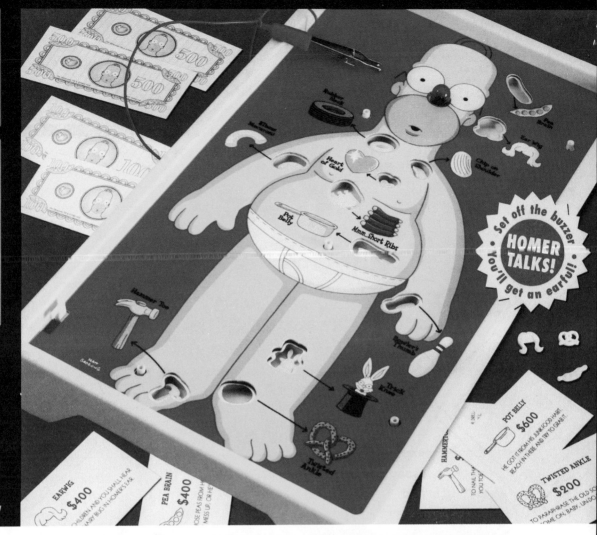

NINTENDO DS™ · THE SIMPSONS GAME

#50105 · Nintendo® · BART SIMPSONS™ ESCAPE FROM CAMP DEADLY · AK™

Licensed by Nintendo for play on the Nintendo® ENTERTAINMENT SYSTEM · THE SIMPSONS™ BART VS. THE SPACE MUTANTS · AK™ · #10503

LICENSED BY Nintendo® · THE SIMPSONS™ BART VS. THE WORLD · AK® · #10505

#10701 · Nintendo® · KRUSTY'S FUN HOUSE · AK®

Nintendo® ENTERTAINMENT SYSTEM® · THE SIMPSONS BARTMAN MEETS RADIOACTIVE MAN · AKlaim

THE SIMPSONS™ BART'S NIGHTMARE · AKlaim

#60111 · VIRTUAL BART · AKlaim entertainment inc.

KRUSTY'S SUPER FUN HOUSE · #60104 · AKlaim entertainment, inc.

PlayStation®2 · THE SIMPSONS Skateboarding · SLUS 20114 · NTSC U/C

PlayStation®2 · THE SIMPSONS ROAD RAGE · FOX · SLUS 20305 · NTSC U/C

PlayStation®2 · THE SIMPSONS HIT & RUN · SLUS 20624 · NTSC U/C

PlayStation®2 · THE SIMPSONS GAME · SLUS 21665 · NTSC U/C

Video Games

JAMES HICKS

Video games! The tool that allows you to vicariously live out your frustrations, sick humor, and knack for causing destruction through the eyes, body, and mind of a digital being. No consequences, but infinite possibilities—and what better characters to insert yourself into than those in *The Simpsons?*

The Simpsons have appeared on almost every video game system, evolving from 8-bit platform gaming to sprawling 3D open worlds. Back in the day, you had to delicately blow the dust off a cartridge or wipe a fingerprint off a CD before inserting it into your big clunky system and praying that it would work. Whereas now you can hang up on Grandma, swipe up on your cell phone, and download a *Simpsons* game to the same device that sits perfectly in your palm.

This interactive expansion of the *Simpsons* universe has evolved into every sort of genre you can think of. You can wrestle, skateboard, bowl, blast aliens, and commit a bit of reckless driving. These video games have varied widely in success and reception, with some games judged "perfectly cromulent," and others as "craptacular."

The magic of *Simpsons* gaming elevated the way fans experienced the show. We can now explore 742 Evergreen Terrace, chat with the eclectic townsfolk, and even kick Ralph Wiggum around like a beach ball (don't lie, we've all done it). In short, we were transported through our TV sets and into the lives of the characters we love most.

In this chapter, we will break down every *Simpsons* game ever released, from the 1991 Konami "beat-'em-up" arcade game, all the way up to *Tapped Out*, released in 2012. We'll be breaking down the plot of each game, along with its trivia, as well as what fans and critics thought of it at the time of release.

The Simpsons Arcade Game

(KONAMI, 1991)

Platform: Arcade

PLOT

The game opens with Waylon Smithers attempting to steal a very large diamond from a jewelry shop. The Simpsons family collides with him, sending the diamond flying into the air, where it lands in the mouth of Maggie Simpson, in place of her pacifier. Smithers then takes Maggie with him, leaving the family to chase after him in search of Maggie.

OVERVIEW

This game is your classic side-scrolling "beat-'em-up"-type arcade game that Konami was well-known for.

The Simpsons Arcade was released during the second season of the show, meaning that the developers only had the Tracy Ullman shorts and the first season to work from. With this in mind, the developers captured Springfield surprisingly well, with the Nuclear Power Plant, Moe's Tavern, and Krustyland providing fun, recognizable backdrops to the violent mayhem on screen. You could take control of either Homer, Marge, Bart, or Lisa, and beat up hordes of goons with a personalized flurry of fists, vacuums, skateboards, or skipping ropes.

The game was a fast-paced button-masher that was best enjoyed with friends on co-op. It did get a little crowded when played with four people, especially with all of you cramped shoulder to shoulder around one arcade machine.

The game was reviewed well by critics and went on to win a platinum award from the American Amusement Machine Association. It was one of the three bestselling games in America the year of its release. The game was also released on the Commodore 64 and MS-DOS computers shortly after the arcade release, as well as PlayStation Network and Xbox Live Arcade several years later in 2012.

In 2021, Arcade1Up released a new, smaller version of the cabinet, also featuring "Simpsons Bowling." It is still a favorite among show and video game fans!

Bart vs. the Space Mutants
(ACCLAIM, 1991)

Platforms: NES, Sega Genesis, Commodore 64, Amiga, Amstrad CPC, Atari ST, ZX Spectrum, Sega Master System, and Sega Game Gear.

PLOT

Aliens have invaded Springfield, and only Bart Simpson knows of their secret plan. Using his special x-ray sunglasses, he has to stop them from collecting the items they need to build their "ultimate weapon" to take over the world.

OVERVIEW

This was the first of many *Simpsons* games focusing solely on Bart. This made sense, as Bartmania was running wild at this point with children across the country shocking parents and teachers alike by wearing his outrageous T-shirts and spouting his catchphrases, like, "Don't have a cow, man!"

Every kid idolized bad boy Bart, and now they got to play as the spikey haired rebel in a video game. So it was no surprise that *Bart vs. the Space Mutants* was a massive hit, selling over a million copies. But despite this financial success, the reviews of the game were mixed at best.

It was criticized due to its almost comical difficulty, having certain requirements to pass each level. You only had a limited number of lives and no continues, so if you ran out, then you started right back at the beginning. Nintendo Power Magazine described the game as "very challenging and could be frustratingly so to some players. The tasks that you must perform to complete the adventure require patience and skill."

It also didn't help that the Nintendo Entertainment System's limited palette of colors didn't include a yellow that matched the *Simpsons* signature skin tone, meaning that Bart's sprite had a sickly green tinge, giving the impression that he'd spent too much time at the Nuclear Power Plant.

The game wasn't without its fans, however. In a 1991 review from *Entertainment Weekly*, Lou Kreston wrote, "What makes it challenging are clever strategic puzzles rather than thumb-bruising acrobatics. *Bart* tests reflexes *and* imagination in a way all too rarely seen in video games."

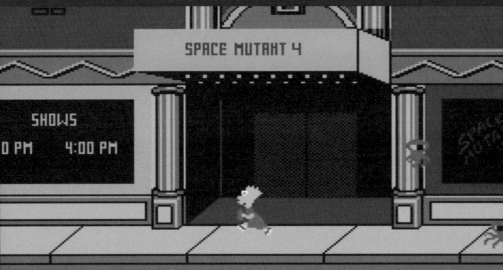

SPACE MUTANT 4

SHOWS

0 PM   4:00 PM

X-RAY SPECS

1200 | 4 | 580 | 23

SCORE   LIVES TIME   GOALS

Bart Simpson's Escape from Camp Deadly (ACCLAIM, 1991)

Platform: Gameboy

PLOT

Bart and Lisa head off to summer camp, which ends up being run by the nephew of Mr. Burns, Ironfist Burns. The game follows Bart as you complete miserable challenges instituted by counselor Burns, and eventually as you try to escape the camp, avoiding counselors, bullies, killer hornets, traps, and more. Eventually, Bart and Lisa switch off the lights of the camp, as they leave for good.

OVERVIEW

This was the first *Simpsons* game released on the portable GameBoy. The game is often noted for its similarities to the episode "Kamp Krusty," which didn't air until a year after the release of the game.

The game received very little praise among critics, and was commonly called "basic" and "uninspired." Some were also critical of its lack of actual tie-ins to the show. November 1991's issue of *GamePro* wrote, "With just three lives and no continues, *The Simpsons Escape from Camp Deadly* [sic] is a tough nut to crack. Then again, Bart's never made anybody's life easy."

A 1992 review in *Games-X* magazine wrote, "The sound is OK with little samples of Bart's own, shrill voice, but the game is pretty dull and at best boring. You may love the annoying character on the TV but I'm afraid you'll probably be disappointed with this latest effort on the Game Boy."

One of the more positive reviews appeared in *Total! UK Magazine*, which gave it a high score of 92/100. "Lucky old Bart seems to star in all the decent carts! Gameplay might be dead simple, but it looks good, sounds good and plays like a dream. Stick at it for a couple of minutes and I guarantee you'll be hooked!"

Bart vs. the World (ACCLAIM, 1991)

Platforms: Amiga, Atari ST, Game Gear, NES, Master System.

PLOT

The game is set up much like the plot of an episode, with Bart going on the Krusty the Clown show and winning a trip around the world as part of a scavenger hunt. We then find out that Smithers has rigged the contest in order for Mr. Burns to get rid of the Simpsons family. Over the course of the game, you encounter and battle many relatives of Burns from different parts of the world.

OVERVIEW

The game has four major areas, China, the North Pole, Egypt, and Hollywood. Within each area there are several stages and minigames to play through. As with every 2D platformer, there are several enemies to dodge and items to collect. The China level, for example, sees you ride down the Great Wall of China on Bart's skateboard as you collect Krusty heads.

Bart vs. the World received mixed reviews, with many comparing it to Bart's previous NES outing. *GamePro* magazine wrote, "After running him through the rigors of a zany-but-strenuous Nintendo workout, the conclusion of this review became obvious: if ya loved Bart in *Bart vs. the*

Space Mutants, you're gonna like him in *Bart vs. the World*."

Some critics praised it for its references, while others referred to the gameplay as "boring." In an issue of *Computer and Video Games*, reviewer Rik Skews wrote, "It's not that it's bad, it's just drab and uninspired. Unless you're a giant fan of *The Simpsons* there's not much here."

Sega Master Force wrote that it's "a good-looking Simpsons adventure with excellent sub-games but lacks lastability."

Bart's House of Weirdness

(KONAMI, 1992)

Platform: MS-DOS

PLOT

Bart is grounded by Homer and Marge, and decides to escape. Along the way, he helps Maggie, explores the basement, and goes to the movies, as well as the Springfield Mall. After leaving the house, he goes around Springfield and eventually to an amusement park, where he saves Krusty the Clown.

OVERVIEW

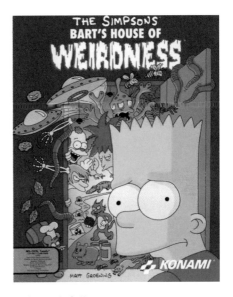

This was a platform game only released for DOS, causing it to have a very narrow fan base despite positive reviews for its graphics, sharp colors, and sound. In a 1992 issue of *Computer Gaming World*, the reviewer wrote, "Graphically, *House of Weirdness* very much resembles *The Simpsons* TV show. The program also includes music taken from the show, as well as digitized samples of the demonic delinquent's famous voice."

A review from a 1992 issue 179 of *Dragon* magazine said, "Without a doubt, *Bart's House of Weirdness* is one of the best arcade games we've played. It also happens to be one of Konami's best products! Our only wish is that Konami would consider releasing this fine arcade delight with full VGA support sometime in the future. If you like Bart and really enjoy arcade games, you have to get this one."

Many believe the game would have been more well received if it was given a broader release. Due to the lack of coverage, and the fact that little gameplay exists available online, many *Simpsons* fans are completely unaware that *Bart's House of Weirdness* even exists.

Krusty's Fun House (ACCLAIM, 1992)

Platforms: NES, SNES, Game Boy, Master System, Game Gear, Genesis, Amiga, DOS.

PLOT

Krusty makes his way through a Krusty Brand fun house, attempting to exterminate pests by leading them through complicated maze-like levels and into traps. Various creatures attempt to complicate Krusty's progress by injuring him. The game also features appearances from Bart, Homer, Corporal Punishment, and Sideshow Mel.

OVERVIEW

There's a recurring joke in *The Simpsons* where Krusty the Clown slaps his Brand Seal of Approval on any piece of crud so long as you drive a "dump truck load of money" to his house. So it's entirely fitting that the first licensed video game that bears his name is simply a reskinned version of an existing game called *Rat Trap* for the Commodore Amiga. The game was licensed to Acclaim, which then adapted it into a game based on Krusty the Clown. The hilarious thing is that we can imagine Krusty doing this exact same thing in the show to save a few bucks.

But, despite sharing the level designs and backgrounds of a preexisting game,

Krusty's Fun House received fairly positive reviews. Unlike his forced labor camp, sorry, I mean, "Kamp Krusty Summer Camp," or his home pregnancy test that "may cause birth defects," *Krusty's Fun House* was surprisingly well received, with many saying it was fun despite the gameplay being simple.

Sega Zone Magazine awarded it a high 90 out of 100 and described it as "the sort of game which I could play for ages." The review went on to say that "*Krusty's Fun House* is one of those games which should appeal to almost everyone."

A 1992 review for the *Sega Genesis Mean Machine Magazine* gave it 90 out of 100, writing, "The graphics and sound are both excellent, but they're really secondary to the gameplay. Puzzle games aren't usually very popular, but I urge you to give this a go. It'll also keep you entertained for weeks—which is more than your average 'big name' platform game will do!"

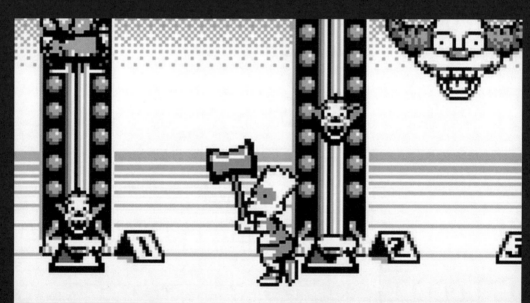

Bart vs. the Juggernauts

(ACCLAIM, 1992)

Platform: Game Boy

PLOT

This game sees Bart competing in a game show where he must complete various challenges, such as an obstacle course at the Kwik-E-Mart, and dodging Dr. Marvin Monroe's electrified tiles. Bart must complete each challenge to progress onto next week's episode of *Juggernauts*.

OVERVIEW

This was the second game released for the Game Boy, again focusing solely on Bart. The game is loosely based on the *American Gladiators* television show.

The game received fairly average reviews, with a few praising the game for its unique concept. Some critics also made note of its *Simpsons*-style humor within the commentary. A 1992 edition of *Hand-Held Go VideoGames* magazine gave the game a score of 74 out of 100, writing, "This cart is a rad laugh from start to finish. Bart's tiny animations are excellent and although there doesn't appear to be much to it you'll be hooked until you've finished."

N-Force magazine described *Bart vs. the Juggernauts* as "not a bad game but not enough options and just too difficult."

Playtime Magazine was a little more critical, writing, "I've played a lot of nasty games, but this thing really sucks in that regard. Either you have to practice this thing for hundreds of years (per discipline, of course) or you have to have an enormous knack, uh, talent. The trappings are done quite well, but the effort (including the sound) was in vain."

The Simpsons: Bartman Meets Radioactive Man (ACCLAIM, 1992)

Platform: NES, Game Gear

PLOT

When Radioactive Man is imprisoned in the Limbo Zone, Bart must save his crimson-clad hero by becoming Bartman. He has to fight Radioactive Man's foes while collecting his stolen powers and returning them to the crimson-clad superhero.

OVERVIEW

This side-scrolling 2D platformer received poor to mixed reception at the time, with a lot of the criticism going toward the stiff and difficult controls. In the fifth issue of *Nintendo Magazine System*, reviewer Andrew wrote, "It would be easy to ignore *Bart* [sic] *Meets Radioactive Man*, and, if you did, you wouldn't miss out on much. But if you can cope with boring graphics and monotone tunes, you have a tough game that should take a while to complete."

A 1992 review in *Electronic Games* said, "In the end, the game has its good moments, but is a flawed product. Bart Simpson-philes will like it, but *Bartman Meets Radioactive Man* is an underachiever, man."

But it was notable for featuring enemies of Radioactive Man who were referenced in the show, as well as the comics, such as Dr. Crab, Magmo the Lava Man, Brain-O, and Swamp Hag. Although Bart's alter ego "Bartman" rarely appeared in the television series, he was featured heavily in merchandise.

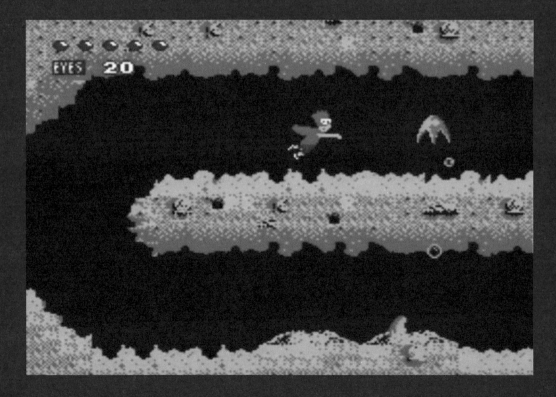

Bart's Nightmare (ACCLAIM, 1992)

Platforms: SNES, Sega Genesis.

PLOT

In this game, Bart falls asleep while studying, leading him into a strange universe in his dream state. It's here that Bart tries to catch up on his homework, opening up a series of portals to different levels where he can transform into Bartman, Indiana Jones, or Godzilla, or even battle diseases within his own bloodstream.

OVERVIEW

Bart's Nightmare is one of the more notoriously challenging *Simpsons* video games ever released. On entering Bart's dreamworld, you arrive on a street that basically serves as the game's hub. Immediately, everything is trying to kill you, like speeding buses, bouncing Jebediah Springfield heads, and even killer mailboxes. You will then have to chase down and catch pages of Bart's homework, which will take you to a minigame ranging from the ridiculously fun to the downright frustrating. Many a child's thumbs were blistered on the Bartman level where you had to maneuver around hazardous Krusty balloons and radioactive clouds and dodge heat-seeking paper airplanes, all the while trying not to be killed by Barney the barfly on a flying pink elephant.

Despite its difficulty, *Bart's Nightmare* had some really imaginative visuals. The sprite-work looked great, and the colors really popped on the 16-bit system. The game received high praise from *N-Force* magazine, which wrote, "Bart Simpson has appeared in lots of games now with varied success, but I can safely say that this is his best adventure yet."

Computer and Video Games wrote, "What more could a Simpsons fan ask for? This game has got the lot. All the best characters, a liberal dose of humor, wanton violence and frequently groovy music."

It turns out that the making of this game was a nightmare itself. *Bart's Nightmare* was programmed by legendary developer Bill Williams, who referred to the game as "Bill's Nightmare." This was because of constant corporate interference that caused Williams to quit midway through the game's production, and even leave the industry altogether to become a pastor.

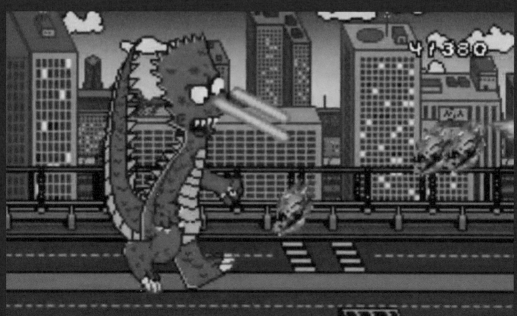

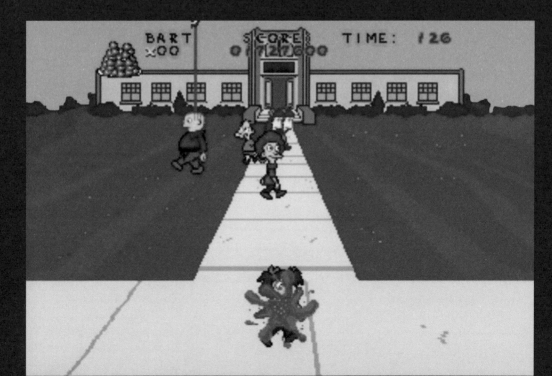

Virtual Bart (ACCLAIM, 1994)

Platform: Super NES, Genesis

PLOT

The story sees Bart at the school science fair, where he becomes trapped in a virtual reality experiment. The only way to escape the machine is to complete all the games on the wheel.

OVERVIEW

Virtual Bart sees you play six mini games, each with variations of Bart, like a dinosaur, a pig, and a baby. The worlds are quite imaginative, with one level seeing Bart traveling on a motorbike through the post-apocalyptic ruins of Springfield, and another seeing you escape Krusty's Pork Factory before you end up on the menu.

The mini games range widely in enjoyability, from terrible to decent

One of the few standouts is the Vandal level, where you throw tomatoes and eggs at your fellow students. You have to aim and time your projectile just right in order to nail oblivious walkers-by. Simple gameplay, but really fun when you get the hang of it.

The animation at the beginning of the game is pretty good for a 16-bit system, and there is variety between the levels. But overall, this is one of the more forgettable early *Simpsons* titles released. *Virtual Bart* received mixed reviews, with *Electronic Gaming Monthly* saying it "just plain misses the mark. The stages are unappealing, and the whole thing seems rushed."

Super Gamer was more positive, giving it an 84/100: "I was constantly amazed by the clarity of the voices, and it all makes *Virtual Bart* a hilarious experience from beginning to end."

The Simpsons: Itchy & Scratchy in Miniature Golf Madness

(ACCLAIM, 1994)

Platform: Game Boy

PLOT

As Scratchy, the player attempts to complete nine miniature golf courses. And, if playing golf on a 2D platformer wasn't difficult enough, you also have to constantly avoid Itchy's attacks. While putting on the green, you have to dodge Itchy's onslaught of grenades, chainsaws, and dynamite.

OVERVIEW

Combining the most relaxing pastime with the violent antics of a cartoon cat and mouse is an interesting choice for a video game, to say the least. The brutal duo Itchy and Scratchy made their debut in the Tracy Ullman short "There's No Disgrace Like Home" in 1990, and they've been a staple in the Simpsons household ever since. Itchy and Scratchy have gone on to have their own movie and a theme park, so a video game featuring the two does make sense.

Their slapstick antics translated well to the video game medium, with *Miniature Golf Madness* capturing their chaotic relationship quite well, although the

developers had to severely tone down the pair's signature violence, given that this game was aimed at children. We must admit, however, that Itchy feeding Scratchy a bowl of his own intestines would have been interesting to see in 8-bit glory.

Itchy & Scratchy in Miniature Golf Madness received positive reviews. *VideoGames & Computer Entertainment* rated it 9 out of 10 and wrote, "You'll never know just how fun miniature golf can be until you play this Itchy and Scratchy game. The unique gameplay sets it apart from other platform games. You get a golf game and an action game all in one."

Jeff Kapalka of the *Syracuse Herald-American* wrote, "The golf game is pretty neat, in and of itself. Throw in the aspect of sudden death—literally—and you've got an exciting, funny cart."

MINIATURE
GOLF MADNESS!

The Simpsons: Bart & the Beanstalk (ACCLAIM, 1994)

Platform: Game Boy

PLOT

The game combines the television series with the classic fairy tale, "Jack and the Beanstalk". The story begins with Bart trading his cow for some magic beans and a slingshot. But before he can plant them, Homer eats the beans, mistaking them for delicious candy. He spits them out, and the next morning Bart wakes up to find a giant beanstalk that stretches toward the heavens. Upon climbing to the top, he finds a castle, as well as a giant that looks suspiciously like Homer.

OVERVIEW

Having a video game focused squarely on a single fairy tale is an odd choice for a premise. But after the previous entries saw us battle space mutants and travel through Bart's dreams, maybe a "Jack and the Beanstalk" retelling isn't so strange in comparison.

It's a straightforward game that sees you climbing up the beanstalk while taking out bugs, using your slingshot. Once you get inside the castle, you'll then have to deal with mice and falling needles. The gameplay is pretty basic and simple, and wouldn't be worth playing without

the *Simpsons* IP attached. Although the graphics were decent by Game Boy standards, Bart's sprite looked pretty good.

Bart & the Beanstalk received mixed to negative reviews from critics. 1994's edition of *Electronic Gaming Monthly* gave it a 5 out of 10, saying, "It's way too hard for the average player, and the younger kids who this is probably aimed at will get frustrated. This game is average at best."

A 1994 reviewer in *Game Players* magazine was less than impressed with the game, writing, "The designers of this action game took a standard story, plastered the Simpsons faces on boring characters, then threw in some of the show's running jokes. Bor-ring!"

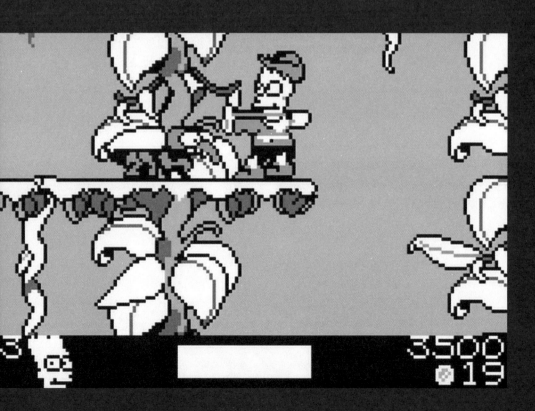

The Itchy & Scratchy Game
(ACCLAIM, 1995)

Platform: Super NES, Game Gear

PLOT

Following the success of *Itchy & Scratchy in Miniature Golf Madness*, Acclaim gave the cat-and-mouse duo another title. But unlike the previous entry, this time you take control of Itchy, and much like the ultra-violent TV show, you have to kill Scratchy any way you can, using giant mallets, bazookas, and chainsaws.

OVERVIEW

Although the game mostly captured the bloodthirsty spirit of the show, *The Itchy & Scratchy Game* was still received poorly, with criticism being aimed toward the repetitive nature of the gameplay and poor controls. 1995's *GamePro* wrote, "The control is the worst part. In a game of

jumping and hitting, the lack of jumping attacks and the inaccurate weapons make you itch for a different game."

Entertainment Weekly wrote, "There's a reason Itchy & Scratchy cartoons rarely occupy more than thirty seconds of any Simpsons episode: stretch the concept to the full half hour, and the ratings would plummet. It's the same for video games.

While Itchy and Scratchy appeared in a hilarious cameo on the Super NES cartridge *Bart's Nightmare*, here they duke it out in an interminable, multistage whackfest."

Game Players Magazine wrote, "Gameplay suffers from extensive repetition and poor control and, despite the large number of weapons included in the game, there are too few opportunities to pick them up. For true Simpsons fans, the Itchy and Scratchy level in *Bart's Nightmare* is still the best place to look for this duo."

The Simpsons: Cartoon Studio
(FOX INTERACTIVE, 1996)

Platform: Microsoft Windows, Mac OS

PLOT

This game allows players to create their own *Simpsons* episodes by using characters, sound effects, locations, dialogue, and music from the series. There are 17 characters, 35 backgrounds, and 250 props to choose from, so you can create your own *Simpsons* shorts.

OVERVIEW

Growing up watching *The Simpsons* as a kid myself, I, and I'm sure many of you reading this now, had always dreamt of working for *The Simpsons* one day. Whether in the animation or writing department, we just wanted to be a part of crafting a *Simpsons* episode in some way. Well, we sorta got our wish with *The Simpsons: Cartoon Studio*, albeit in a very crude and janky way. This PC program allowed us to craft our own *Simpsons* stories to show our friends and family. These shorts were never good, mind you, near unwatchable in fact, but nonetheless we all felt just like Matt Groening.

The game was mostly positively received despite its laggy limitations. Joseph Szadkowski of the *Washington Times* wrote, "For the amount of complicated computer stuff going on—frame by frame editing, character motion, voice overlays—even the most computer-illiterate individual should be able to figure this out. *The Simpsons: Cartoon Studio* is a very fun, relatively inexpensive jaunt into the mind of Mr. Groening."

The 1996 issue of MacHome magazine rated the game four apples out of five. "Overall, *The Simpsons: Cartoon Studio*'s performance is smooth. Once you've got it all together, it plays back as cleanly as a Sunday night episode. You can even save your cartoon to a self-playing file you can send someone, who won't need the *Cartoon Studio* program to see it."

The Simpsons: Virtual Springfield (FOX INTERACTIVE, 1997)

Platform: Windows, Macintosh

PLOT

Explore 3D Springfield in this point-and-click adventure game. In it, you can explore the various locations seen in the show, like the Simpsons' house, Moe's Tavern, and Springfield Elementary, to name a few. You can also interact with the town's eclectic residents and play mini games at Noiseland Arcade.

The overall goal is to unlock secret areas within the map and collect an entire set of character cards throughout Springfield.

OVERVIEW

Despite the constant threat of nuclear meltdowns and the likelihood of growing a third eye from drinking its polluted water, most of us have thought of what it would be like to visit Springfield. In many ways, Evergreen Terrace was a second home to us. Who hasn't thought of visiting the Kwik-E-Mart and chatting it up with Apu over a Squishee, or browsing through the latest issue of *Radioactive Man* at The Android's Dungeon & Baseball Card Shop.

At the time, *Virtual Springfield* was the closest we could get to exploring

Springfield. The game allowed us to catch the latest McBain flick at the Aztec Theater and watch a secret meeting at the Stonecutters Lodge. There are a lot of Easter eggs and references throughout the game for both casual and hardcore *Simpsons* fans.

The game received mixed reviews, with many commenting on the repetitive nature of the gameplay. A 1997 review from *Billboard* newsletter wrote, "Unfortunately, the detail is so great that there are moments when *Virtual Springfield* can become somewhat tedious."

A more positive review can be found in a 1997 issue of *Electronic Games*. "Bottom Line: Fans of *The Simpsons* should enjoy this game very much. Interface is a little confusing, and a few key locations could not be explored. There are references to almost every episode of the show, very well done."

The Simpsons Bowling (KONAMI, 2000)

Platform: Arcade

PLOT

This game starts off with the Nuclear Power Plant having a meltdown in Sector 7G, and on Homer's chair sits a sign that reads "Gone Bowling." That is the extent of the story. The player can choose from nine *Simpsons* characters, each with its own specific statistics, with the aim being to knock down as many pins as possible. The game has distinct endings, depending on who you played as. For example, if you won the game as Lisa, she would proceed to laugh maniacally until she transformed into Kang.

OVERVIEW

Having a *Simpsons* game focused squarely on bowling made complete sense. It is Homer's favorite sport, after all, and bowling has been the central focus of a few episodes, most notably, season seven's "Team Homer," which saw the creation of the Pin Pals, with Homer, Moe, Apu, and Mr. Burns.

The purple arcade cabinet design replicated a grimy bowling alley, with spilled ketchup, donut crumbs, and coffee stains printed on it. The signature of "El Barto" was also scratched into the surface. It's a great-looking arcade machine that unfortunately is quite rare to find today. But if you're lucky enough to find one, then it may set you back at least $3,500.

The gameplay was pretty simple, with just a trackball you use to aim, angle, and curve the ball. You can play as Bart, Lisa, Homer, Marge, Mr. Burns, Apu, Willie, or Krusty the Clown. And if you're wondering where Maggie is, she is in the game, but only as a bowling ball, once you score a turkey. Each character had its own unique dialogue after its turn; for example, after getting a spare, Homer would say, "In your face, stupid pins!"

Each character had its own ending, which made you want to sink all your quarters in and watch each one. Mr. Burns's ending sees the billionaire tycoon struggle to lift his trophy before Maggie pops out. This terrifies Monty, who cowers on the floor, which makes sense, as it was the baby who shot him. Apu's ending sees him celebrating until Mr. Burns drops in, pointing a gun at the convenience store clerk before taking off with his trophy.

While not as well-known as Konami's first outing, the game was well-loved in arcades across the country. *The Simpsons Bowling* was recently given a second life when it was added as a secondary game to Arcade 1Up's home arcade machine, released in 2021.

WAIT FOR GREEN

FRAME

10

Night of the Living Treehouse of Horror (THQ, 2001)

Platform: Game Boy Color

PLOT

Based on the annual Halloween specials, this 2D side-scroller adventure recreates classic segments from the Treehouse of Horror episodes. There are seven levels to complete, with level one being based on Bad Dream House from the first Treehouse special. Level two is based on "Fly vs. Fly" from "Treehouse of Horror VIII." And level three is based on the segment "Dial 'Z' For Zombies" from "Treehouse of Horror III."

OVERVIEW

The annual Treehouse of Horror specials allowed the writers to get as creatively weird and dark as possible without worrying about the implications in future episodes. Thus Mr. Burns can be Dracula, and Bart can transform into a fly. So having a video game based on the many imaginative Treehouse of Horror segments was a great idea.

Night of the Living Treehouse of Horror was a significant improvement over the previous Nintendo handheld entries. With this being the first *Simpsons* title on the Game Boy Color, the vibrant backgrounds and sprites really popped on the 2.6-inch screen.

This game received fairly decent reviews. Frank Provo of *GameSpot* gave the game a 7.8 out of 10 and wrote that "each level is a game unto itself, which makes for a rather pleasing and varied experience," before going on to say that it's "colorfully drawn, highly detailed, and smoothly animated."

Gamezone awarded it an 8 out of 10 and wrote, "As GameBoy Color games go, this title is great. It is fun to play, has decent graphics and the levels are challenging without being ridiculous."

The Simpsons Wrestling

(ELECTRONIC ARTS, ACTIVISION, 2001)

Platform: Playstation

PLOT

Unlike the others previously mentioned, there isn't much story given within this game, but the manual provides an entertaining outline from Kent Brockman himself. He reports that Springfield has been gripped by "wrestling fever" brought on by "an alien force." Therefore, the town's residents "have been challenged by wrestling rivals from another planet." You may be unsurprised to learn that this otherworldly duo is none other than Kang and Kodos, who you go face-to-giant-eye with at the end of the game. In the game, there are eighteen playable characters, each with its own exclusive moves and gestures.

OVERVIEW

Professional wrestling was massive in the early 2000s, both on television and consoles, with WWE, WCW, and ECW all bringing out their own gaming titles during the period. Seeing the popularity of pro wrestling explode, EA wanted to get in on the trend. And what better way to cash in on the wrestling game market than by using Simpsons IP—from a cartoon not known for its wrestling in any way? So, predictably, like a chairshot to the back

of the head, *The Simpsons Wrestling* crashed hard upon release.

Players complained about its janky controls and poor graphics. Other common complaints were the lack of wrestling moves, which is something one would expect in a wrestling game.

In fact, it's often regarded as not only the worst *Simpsons* game ever, but also one of the worst games of all time!

GamePro magazine described it as "a 'game' that's awful in every respect and will ultimately be a textbook example of a wasted license." IGN gave the game a dismal 1 out of 10, and declared it "the most horrific demolition of a license ever." Ouch!

But a lot of the blame for the game's critical failure may come down to studio interference. The developers were huge *Simpsons* fans and truly set out to make a great *Simpsons* game. In fact, the developers wrote most of the dialogue themselves, sending their script drafts to the studio, believing that the *Simpsons* writers would either edit what they wrote, or completely start over fresh. But when the developing team got the recordings back, they were surprised to find that the voice actors read *their* scripts word for word. Ray West, who was the 3D modeler and animator for *Simpsons Wrestling*, explained, "It was a miracle. We got the raw takes and I remember Hank Azaria busted up laughing at some line one of us wrote. We peaked at our careers."

The developers did receive some recordings written by *Simpsons* staff, but unfortunately some didn't make it to the final game. Level Designer Michael Ebert said in an interview, "We had our testers come back to us and say, you know, the dialogue in *The Simpsons Wrestling* game is so offensive I'll never allow my child to play it. And we had to cut out a large number of the things they said. So there are a whole bunch of *Simpsons* recorded lines by the voice actors that just never saw the light of day."

Also, according to Ebert, FOX required that black lines be drawn around the characters. He said, "We were just going to do 3D rendered characters without the little black cartoon line and putting that black line on there killed a lot of the performance." Supposedly, this addition was incredibly taxing on the PlayStation,

and so they were forced to change the rendering and lower the resolution. However, you can remove the black lines yourself in the settings and play the way the developers intended.

The developers also believed that their title didn't help reviews either. Ebert said, "My only real problem with that game is that I just think it should never have been called wrestling. It should have been *Simpsons Brawl* or something." The developers believed that people were expecting a pro wrestling game with professional wrestling moves. Instead of chokeslams and piledrivers, wrestling enthusiasts instead got slapstick shenanigans, like Krusty with a giant mallet and Marge with a frying pan.

The developers were also told to remove many fun and innovative features, such as interactive character "select screens" where they could reach across to punch and trash-talk each other. This sounds like a really funny and creative idea. But the devs were told to remove these and replace them with static 2D images of the characters instead.

Although the removed dialogue, features, and title change might not have *totally* saved the game, it is interesting to look back and wonder if the game would have been better if the dev team were given more creative freedom. But as it stands, *The Simpsons Wrestling* will go down as one of the biggest blunders in video game history.

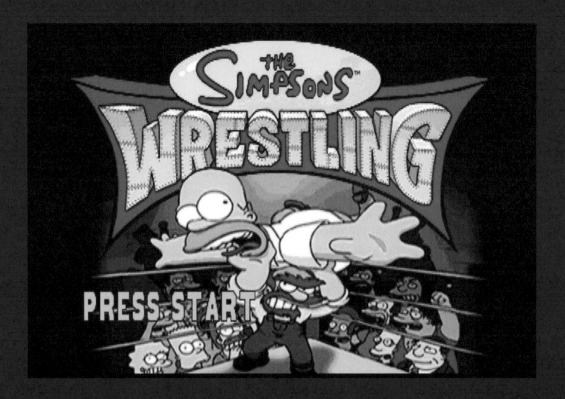

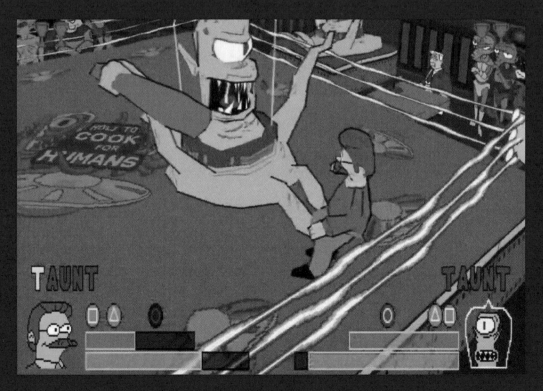

PRESS START

The Simpsons: Road Rage

(ELECTRONIC ARTS, 2001)

Platform: PS2, Xbox, GameCube and Game Boy Advance

PLOT

In the game, Mr. Burns has bought all transit systems in Springfield and has begun to create radioactive buses that threaten the public's health. Because of this, the citizens of Springfield must use their own cars as a means of safer public transport and earn money in an attempt to pay back Burns to get rid of the radioactive buses and return the town to normal.

OVERVIEW

The game was an obvious rip-off of Sega's *Crazy Taxi*, with the goal being to pick up and get your passengers to their destinations in the quickest way possible before the time limit ran out. Along the way, you can destroy property and run over your least favorite characters. The developers of *Road Rage* are very open and honest about the fact that the game was heavily "inspired" by *Crazy Taxi*. Nathan Sutter, test lead on *The Simpsons: Road Rage* said in an interview, "It did start out as just a *Crazy Taxi* rip-off, but it was also full of fan service. The game did fan service really, really well and that's what the fans loved."

Matt Groening was heavily involved in the creative process of this game. In an interview with inverse.com, John Melchior, producer of the game, said, "One of the biggest highlights of the whole thing was getting to watch Matt Groening test out the game. For about two hours once a month, we'd go to his office and he'd play the game, his son would play, and we'd have two guys in the corner taking notes. I remember seeing the wonderment in his eyes when he was driving the Homer car and I heard him laugh at the game. He was such a great creative partner."

The reviews for the game were mixed at best, with many praising the voice acting and writing, while criticizing the gameplay and long loading times. *Electronic Gaming Monthly* wrote, "You'll still have to deal with irritating load times and janky collision detection problems (it's easy to get your car stuck on objects and buildings)."

The graphics looked pretty great, and it was fun driving around Springfield in Homer's beat-up pink sedan. With a varied choice of characters and vehicles, there are numerous callbacks to the show, like the Mr. Plow truck, the Canyonero, Snake's Little Bandit, and Apu's Pontiac Firebird. Although dialogue and sound effects were great, they could get repetitive quickly, to the point where my sibling and I could recite word for word every single character's lines. I can't tell you how many times we repeated Ralph's "Your car smells like cat food."

Due to the repetitive nature of the gameplay, it could get monotonous within a couple of hours. As such, the game was best enjoyed in multiplayer, as you each race to pick up the passenger first and chase each other down to steal them.

Due to its many similarities to the Crazy Taxi franchise, Sega filed a lawsuit with FOX Interactive, Electronic Arts, and Radical Entertainment in 2003. Sega alleged the game was designed to "deliberately copy and imitate" Crazy Taxi, which involves racing to get passengers to destinations as quickly as possible. The case, *Sega of America, Inc. vs. FOX Interactive, et al.*, was settled in private mediation for an undisclosed amount.

Despite being derivative of Sega's *Crazy Taxi*, it was a huge success, going platinum and selling over 5.6 million units in the United States by July 2006.

The Simpsons Skateboarding
(ELECTRONIC ARTS, 2002)

Platform: Playstation 2

PLOT

Springfield has been converted into a skateboard for the annual "Skate Tour." With nine playable characters, including Professor Frink for some reason, you can grind, kickflip, and ollie around Springfield.

OVERVIEW

Just as the previous two entries tried to capitalize on the success of other game franchises, *The Simpsons Skateboarding* latched onto the success of the Tony Hawk Pro Skater series. But just like a failed flip trick, this entry was a total wipeout. Much like *The Simpsons Wrestling*, this game was poorly received due to its unresponsive controls and terrible graphics. Most of the skating moves never worked, so you spent more time sprawled on the floor than up in the air.

Along with *The Simpsons Wrestling*, *The Simpsons Skateboarding* is also regarded as one of the worst games ever made. *Game Informer* magazine gave it an abysmal 1 out of 10, writing, "Never before have I seen a developer put forth such an effort to secure the Worst Game of the Year award. I'll even go as far to say that this may very well be the worst PlayStation 2 game on the market."

Kevin Murphy of *GameSpy* said, "*The Simpsons Skateboarding* should be a case study in bad game design." He also went on to say, "If you like *The Simpsons* and love skateboarding, you'll still hate this awful game… One of the worst games of 2002."

GameSpy gave it a low score of 18 out of 100. "There's nothing new or innovative about this game. It doesn't even hit the average mark in terms of fun. If it didn't have the *Simpsons* license this game would have nothing going for it at all. As it stands now, even the *Simpsons* license can't save this game from itself. *The Simpsons Skateboarding* is one of the worst games of 2002."

Martin Taylor of Eurogamer.net wrote, "*Simpsons Skateboarding* is a cash-in in the purest sense of the term. There are barely any redeeming features, it's practically devoid of any humor, the graphics, levels and physics are terrible, and it simply exhausts any entertainment value it does harbour in about five minutes flat."

Press START Button

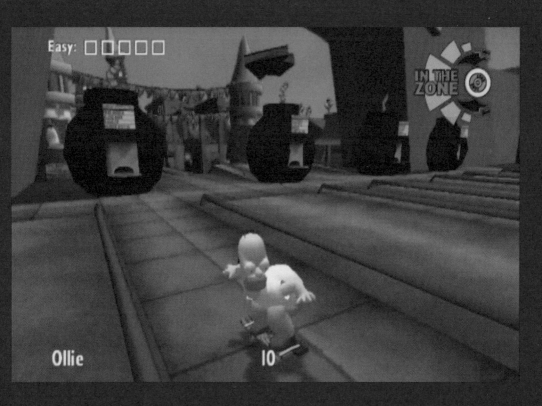

Easy: ☐☐☐☐☐

IN THE ZONE

Ollie

10

The Simpsons: Hit & Run

(VIVENDI GAMES, 2003)

Platform: PS2, Xbox, GameCube and Microsoft Windows

PLOT

In the story of *The Simpsons: Hit & Run*, a new Buzz Cola is released in Springfield, but pretty soon, strange events occur. Surveillance wasps invade the town, and Bart is abducted by aliens. So, playing as the Simpsons family, you have to investigate around Springfield and find out what is happening.

OVERVIEW

Unabashedly inspired by the *Grand Theft Auto* series, *The Simpsons Hit & Run* is a far tamer, family-friendly take on the ultra-violent, carjacking games. Granted, you can still run over pedestrians, but instead of splattering them all over the road, here they just roll over pathetically...which is arguably a lot funnier.

The Simpsons Hit & Run is an open-world driving game where you take control of your favorite characters, complete missions, and explore the town of Springfield. The game even rewards you for creating as much havoc as possible by destroying town property, and kicking innocent bystanders. And I have to say that there was something quite satisfying about beating "stupid sexy Flanders" repeatedly.

Hit & Run was a huge success and received almost universal praise from audiences and critics.

A huge part of the game's success is due to the clever writing and jokes, which were all very in keeping with the humor of the show. *Hit & Run*'s story was penned by show writers Matt Warburton, Tim Long, and Matt Selman. As such, the game was littered with countless references and Easter eggs to classic episodes. Outside of completing missions, you could explore the open world of Springfield, where you can walk into the Kwik-E-Mart and marvel at the amazing Frostillicus, or travel to see the beloved Lemon Tree that marks Springfield's town pride.

Selling over three million copies, and winning numerous awards, it is considered the greatest *Simpsons* game ever by many fans.

PRESS START

The Simpsons Game
(ELECTRONIC ARTS, 2007)

Platform: PS2, PS3, Xbox 360, Nintendo DS, and Wii

PLOT

In this very meta storyline, the Simpsons family realize that they are in a video game, and must search for the creator. Gaining unique special abilities, they must battle through sixteen levels until they ultimately have a showdown with God himself.

OVERVIEW

After numerous releases like *Bart Meets Radioactive Man* and *Virtual Bart*, it is odd that it took over a decade to finally get a game simply called *The Simpsons Game*.

Following the massive success of *Hit & Run*, another *Simpsons* video game was highly anticipated. Although many fans wanted a direct sequel, we were just happy we were finally getting another *Simpsons* game after so long.

One of the best things about *The Simpsons Game* is that it has traditionally animated cutscenes, making it feel more like an interactive episode. The writing is very self-referential and quick-witted, which makes sense when you realize that the game was interspersed with exclusive cutscenes written by *Simpsons* alumni Tim Long and Matt Warburton.

The levels are really imaginative and call back to classic *Simpsons* moments, like Homer frolicking through the Land of Chocolate from season three's "Burns Verkaufen der Kraftwerk." There's even a level where you kick porpoise behind, which was inspired by "Treehouse of Horror XI's Night of the Dolphin." The whole game is a treat for *Simpsons* fans, with tons of references, winks, and nods throughout the entire playthrough.

While not as well received as its predecessor, *Hit & Run*, it was nonetheless a critical and commercial success, selling over four million copies. Despite the game's popularity, a sequel was canceled in 2011, and so far there hasn't been a *Simpsons* game released on console since.

Tapped Out

(EA MOBILE, 2012)

Platform: iOS and Android

PLOT

Tapped Out is a "free to play" village simulator, where the player must help rebuild Springfield after a meltdown at the Nuclear Power Plant causes the entire city to be destroyed. The player can unlock houses, business, and characters, and arrange Springfield however they wish.

OVERVIEW

The gameplay is pretty simple. You start with a clear patch of ground and start dropping in locations from the show. Then you tap the buildings and bundles of XP and dollars pop out, which you then use to buy more properties. Some fans have meticulously recreated Springfield as shown in the show in order to make an exact replica of the town's layout, while others have taken the complete opposite approach and said "To hell with accuracy" by dropping their buildings wherever they damn well please. You can invite other players to visit your town, and seeing your friends place the Flanders House right next to Barney's Bowlarama is enough to make any OCD Simpson fan itch with irritation.

Although they are uncredited, several of the show's writers worked on the game, such as Matt Selman, Matt Warburton, and Brian Kelley, to name a few.

Although *Tapped Out* is free to download, players can purchase in-game items using real-world cash. This has drawn criticism by some for being exploitative and lacking in gameplay. To progress within the game, you complete character quests and levels, but the wait time for some of these tasks can be as long as ninety days. The ridiculously tedious wait times really encourage the player to pay real money for virtual donuts, which can then be swapped for virtual currency.

Tapped Out was a huge success immediately upon launch and was number one in the App Store in fifty-four countries. In 2013, it was revealed that *The Simpsons: Tapped Out* had 5.4 million daily active players. The game continues to be a huge success even today, receiving over eighty million downloads and grossing $200 million as of 2020.

Other Simpsons Video Games

While *The Simpsons Video Game* was the last stand-alone Simpsons title released to consoles, we did get another chance to visit a digital Springfield in *LEGO Dimensions* released in 2015. While not exclusively a *Simpsons* video game, I thought it was important to highlight, as it does contain an entire level dedicated to the animated show. You could also purchase a Simpsons Level Pack and Fun Packs, which contained mini-LEGO figurines of Homer, Bart, and Krusty the Clown.

The Simpsons also released a couple of mobile phone games over the years, including *Minutes to Meltdown* (2005), and *Itchy & Scratchy Land* (2008).

But well before the invention of the cell phone, there were the self-contained handheld games. The first of which was *The Simpsons Electronic LCD Game* released in 1990, making it the first Simpsons video game ever made. The gameplay was obviously basic, with you playing as Bart and dodging obstacles on a skateboard.

Between 1990 and 1999, a number self-contained handheld games were released:

The Simpsons Electronic LCD Game (1990, Tiger Electronics)
The Simpsons Electronic Wrist LCD Game (1990, Tiger Electronics)
Bartman: Avenger of Evil (1990, Acclaim)
Bart Simpson's Cupcake Crisis (1991, Acclaim)
Bart vs. the Space Mutants LCD handheld (1991, Acclaim)
Bart vs. Homersaurus (1994, Tiger Electronics)
The Simpsons LCD (1999, Tiger Electronics)

HAND-HELD ELECTRONIC VIDEO GAME

BARTMAN
AVENGER OF EVIL

MAT GROENING

Maim
inment, inc.

Ages 5 and up

atteries, not included

BARTMAN
AVENGER OF EVIL

The Simpsons™ and Bartman™ TM & © 1990 Twentieth Century Fox
Film Corporation. All rights reserved.

25800

SOUND ON/OFF   SELECT

START/JUMP

ACL

ROW

RIGHT

GRAB

**WE RECOMMEND
ALKALINE BATTERIES**

TALKING

THE SIMPSONS

BART vs HOMERSAURUS

MODEL 7-626
For Ages 5 and above

TIGER
ELECTRONICS INC.
ELECTRONIC LCD GAME

ELECTRONIC

TALKING
THE **SIMPSONS**
BART vs HOMERSAURUS

EEP!

- Watch out! Bart and Lisa are in
  an adventure with radioactive
  dinosaurs!
- Really cool sound effects!
  Bart and Lisa actually talk!
- Watch out for Homersaurus! He's
  half man, half mutant dinosaur!

FEATURING THE
REAL VOICES
OF BART & LISA

CHAPTER NINE: VIDEO GAMES

257

THE SIMPSONS

from *The Simpsons* episode "Homer's Barbershop Quartet"

Fifth Season Premiere Thursday, September 30 (8:00-8:30PM ET/PT) on FOX

"BABY ON BOARD"
(H. Simpson)
THE BE SHARPS

CERTIFIED
★★ HIT ★★

Presented to
THE BE SHARPS
in recognition of
the musical contribution this
'Fab Four' has made with
their hit
'BABY ON BOARD'
(which has sold a whole bunch of records)

THE BE SHARPS

FOR KIDS OVER 3, MAN!

CHAPTER TEN

Music

LYDIA HICKS

Music was always important to Matt Groening when creating *The Simpsons*, from briefing Danny Elfman for the *Simpsons* theme song to head-hunting Alf Clausen to be the show's long-term composer.

Clausen's background in orchestrating TV drama slotted perfectly into Groening's ideal of *The Simpsons* being a "drama in animation," but that's not to say that the composer didn't have his doubts before committing to the show. Animated TV was not a prestigious genre, and no one could have predicted the sophisticated animated phenomenon the show would become. So Clausen only had Groening's pitch to go on: "We don't look upon this as being a cartoon, but a drama where the characters are drawn, and we would like it scored that way." With this brief came musical scores that went beyond what animation had ever done.

Therefore, when *The Simpsons* was unleashed on the world, we were given not only a cleverly written and hilarious cartoon, but stories surrounding a strangely relatable family with all the domestic, economical, and ethical issues we face. Our absorption of these stories was only elevated by the show's musical score. For instance, Marge's rendition of "You Are So Beautiful to Me" in season two's "Simpson and Delilah," as she settles Homer's insecurities is enough to make the strongest of us crumble to the ground.

But it wasn't all tears and heartfelt moments. We were also treated to full-on Broadway belters from Lyle Lanley's "Monorail Song" to Mr. Burns's "See My Vest." As such, it came as no surprise that, along with the hundreds of other merchandising deals, a *Simpsons* album was on the way too. And so commenced the weird and wonderful world of *Simpsons* music merchandise.

The Simpsons Sing the Blues

Released: December 4, 1990
Format: Cassette, CD, LP
Label: Geffen

The Simpsons Sing the Blues was *The Simpsons*'s first album. The idea for its production came from David Geffen, founder of Geffen Records, and was then approved by FOX and Matt Groening. It is interesting to note that this is the only album originally released in the LP format, and consisted of entirely original songs separate from the show—all except for the first verse of "Moaning Lisa Blues," which was first featured in the episode "Moaning Lisa."

Mike Reiss, writer and co-showrunner for *The Simpsons* during seasons three and four, mentioned that James L. Brooks penned the title *The Simpsons Sing the Blues* as a parody of Diana Ross's *Lady Sings the Blues*. And what started out as a funny joke set the genre for the whole project, for the writers were now given the difficult task of writing an album of humorous songs, but for blues and hip-hop melodies.

Even though the genre choice may have started as a simple joke, it actually fed into Bart Simpson's growing prominence in African American culture, as indicated by the growing demand for "Black Bart" bootleg merchandise. As mentioned earlier, Matt Groening embraced this acceptance for his character ("Bart is like Santa Claus. No one really knows what color he is"), and so decided that it was important for Bart, in particular, to perform in a hip-hop style for the album. So, in collaboration with *The Fresh Prince of Bel-Air*'s DJ Jazzy Jeff, Groening wrote "Deep, Deep Trouble," a rap that told the story of Bart's rebellious ways, from snoozing his alarm, throwing secret house parties, to getting punished with awful haircuts and household chores.

There were many other notable musicians rumored to have appeared during the album's production, such as B. B. King, Dr. John, Marcy Levy, and even Michael Jackson. The appearance of such stars only heightened anticipation of the album and made for great press in a world craving more and more of *The Simpsons*.

The album was recorded in September 1990, and released on December 4 of that year. It proved a huge success, peaking at number three on the Billboard 200, making it the highest-charting *Simpsons* album. The album really excelled in the United Kingdom, reaching number six

on the albums chart, and was eventually certified gold. On December 14, 1990, the album was certified platinum, having sold over one million copies in its first week of release. Within a matter of weeks, the record was certified double platinum by the Recording Industry Association of America, on February 13, 1991, for sales of over two million copies.

0 5439-19004-7 0

GEF 87
5439-19004-7 (N)
FRANCE WE 171

Side One • Do The Bartman
(7" House Mix/Edit)

Side Two • Do The Bartman
(LP Edit)

Produced, Written and Mixed by Bryan Loren
for Left Handed Productions
Engineered by Bryan Loren and Richard Cottrell
Remixed by Bryan Loren

Original version from the album
"The Simpsons Sing The Blues"

Do The Bartman

Released: November 20, 1990
Format: Cassette, CD, 7-Inch Vinyl
Label: Geffen

Out of the entirety of *The Simpsons*'s musical career, "Do the Bartman" was certainly its most iconic moment. The success of the single from *The Simpsons Sing the Blues* was a testament to the impact of Bartmania, seeing as it was, in actuality, a cute novelty song, rapped by a cartoon character. But we cannot deny that Nancy Cartwright did a great job in her performance, balanced with a smooth and funky backup track produced by Bryan Loren and the King of Pop himself, Michael Jackson... although the debate as to who specifically wrote it is ongoing.

According to Groening, on the DVD audio commentary for *The Simpsons: The Complete Third Season*, Jackson reached out to express his love for the show, and Bart in particular. So he proposed writing a "number one hit" for the prankster, offering to also guest-star on the show.

One thing we can confirm is that Jackson did guest-star, appearing in season three's premiere "Stark Raving Dad" under the pseudonym "John Jay Smith" as seen in the credits. Here, Jackson/Smith played Leopold, a patient at a mental health facility who believed himself to be Michael Jackson. It was also in this episode that he wrote the equally catchy song, "Happy Birthday, Lisa."

However, this might have been where Jackson's involvement ended. Bryan Loren, the reported original writer of "Do the Bartman" has said that Michael Jackson didn't have any hand in writing the song, just the backing vocals.

"The story of the song and its creation has been a thorn in my side since I did it. But, despite Matt Groening's repeated confessions, I am the sole writer of the song," Loren told *Music Business Worldwide*. "While it's true, along with me, Michael Jackson does sing backing vocals. And it *was* his idea to name the song, 'Do the Bartman,' And he did insist I include his name in the lyric: *If you can do the Bart, you're bad like Michael Jackson... Eat your heart out, Michael! Woop!*"

Many believed Jackson's involvement had to be covered up as he was under contract with Sony Music, and this track was released by Geffen. Groening further confused matters in 1998, when he told an audience of *Simpsons* fans, "It was always amazing to me that no one ever found out that Michael Jackson wrote that song."

Despite confusion, *The Simpsons* still had a major hit on their hands, topping the charts in Australia, Ireland, New Zealand, Norway, and the United Kingdom, while also reaching the top ten in Belgium, Denmark, Finland, the Netherlands, Spain, and Sweden. But even though

"Do The Bartman" had a lot of radio airplay in the United States, it was never officially released as a single there.

FUN FACT: THE MUSIC VIDEO WAS DIRECTED BY THE FUTURE DIRECTOR OF THE INCREDIBLES AND THE IRON GIANT, BRAD BIRD, AND WAS RELEASED IN 1991. IT PREMIERED AFTER THE AIRING OF "BART THE DAREDEVIL" BEFORE BECOMING EXCLUSIVE TO MTV. THE VIDEO WAS AN INSTANT HIT, RECEIVING A NOMINATION AT THE 1991 MTV VIDEO MUSIC AWARDS.

In fact, the frenzy was so strong that the single of "Do the Bartman" was released in four distinct versions:

> "DO THE BARTMAN" (7" HOUSE MIX/EDIT)3:54
> "DO THE BARTMAN" (LP EDIT)3:59
> "DO THE BARTMAN" (BAD BART HOUSE MIX)4:49
> "DO THE BARTMAN" (A CAPPELLA)3:44

My personal favorite is the "House Mix," which was the preferred version for radio play. The "LP edit" and "Bad Bart" have more cameos from the other family members, but I will admit that the a capella version is an acquired taste.

The Yellow Album

Released: November 24, 1998
Format: Cassette, CD
Label: Geffen

The Yellow Album was *The Simpsons*'s second album of originally recorded songs, with the title now parodying the Beatles' highly popular self-titled 1968 album, commonly known as the *White Album.*

The cover art was done by Bill Morrison, satirizing the cover of the Beatles' 1967 album *Sgt. Pepper's Lonely Hearts Club Band,* created by pop artists Peter Blake and Jann Haworth. There are various conscious choices made to link the two albums: The Ullman version of the Simpsons stands alongside the newer version of the family, similarly to the way the 1964 suit-styled Beatles stood alongside their updated and flamboyant selves. Where Marilyn Monroe stood now stands Lurleen Lumpkin, the country music star who attempted to seduce Homer. Wiggum's police hat matched up with Marlon Brando's, and the nuclear drum taking center stage replaced the Beatles' drum in the center.

Morrison's art was so popular that it was used for a couch gag in season eight's "Bart After Dark," and was later redrawn, and color-corrected, for season twenty-seven's "Every Man's Dream."

Like the cover, the music also showcased Springfield's wealth of characters. There were songs from Apu, Otto, and Patty and Selma, such as Lisa and the Bouvier twins' rendition of "Sisters Are Doing It for Themselves." Whereas before the light shone squarely on Bart, it was now shared amongst other characters as the seasons and stories rolled.

But the one song that I would *really* recommend playing on a first date (please sense the sarcasm) is "Twenty-Four Hours A Day" by Apu and The Squishies: "Hello, baby. It is Apu to whom you are speaking. What's that, baby? You are proposing we have a cookout at the beach then tear a page from the Kama Sutra 'til the sun rises over the Eastern Sea? Sorry, baby. That's impossible. I run a convenience store, and baby, you know what that's like."

Then, after a detailed account of his working day, the shop's produce, and his failing American dream, the song concludes with him getting robbed: "Please, sir, I ask that if you tie me up, you use the nylon rope; it feels so much softer against my skin than the other kind. Yes, you'll find it in between the video games and the non-dairy creamer. Please, sir, oh, thank you very much. Okay, have a nice day! Come again!"

It is a roller coaster of emotions, but nonetheless a musical journey that I highly suggest you embark on.

This is why I am sad that these originally written musical numbers were not continued after this. The original songs opened up a whole new side to Springfield, one that was equally well-written and hilarious. Unfortunately, these positives didn't translate into record sales, as the album did not perform as well as its predecessor.

The date of the album's release may have contributed to its lesser success. In 1997, there was a reported drop of *Simpsons* merchandise production in the approach to the millennium. So with that came the soundtrack albums: *Songs in the Key of Springfield*, *Go Simpsonic with The Simpsons*, and *Testify*.

The Simpsons Soundtrack Albums (1997 TO 2007)

By the time *Songs in the Key of Springfield* was released in March 1997, Alf Clausen, along with his thirty-five-piece orchestra, had created an impressive repertoire of musical numbers, from "Baby on Board" by The Be Sharps to Mr. Burns's "See My Vest." Therefore, it made sense economically that *The Simpsons* would eventually have their own soundtrack albums moving away from creating originally recording, and expensive, songs.

Even though it was an intelligent business move, I feel what made the previous albums, with original songs, so special was that they opened up another part of Springfield.

However, even if these albums did not contain original music, they were still great merchandise celebrating all that Alf Clausen was able to achieve over the show's run. Collectively, on all three albums, there are 133 songs, all of which were predominantly composed by Clausen—not counting the musical score that runs underneath the normal dialogue. Overall, the albums honored all of the musical success during what many consider "*The Simpsons*'s Golden Age," and beyond.

The Simpsons: Testify

Released: September 18, 2007
Format: CD, digital download
Label: Shout! Factory

Songs in the Key of Springfield

Released: March 18, 1997
Format: Cassette, CD

Go Simpsonic with The Simpsons

Released: November 2, 1999
Format: Cassette, CD

The Simpsons Movie: The Music

Released: July 24, 2007
Format: CD, digital download
Label: Adrenaline Music Group

When the highly anticipated *The Simpsons Movie* was being developed, producer James L. Brooks chose German film composer Hans Zimmer to take control of the film's score. Zimmer's other Hollywood successes include *Inception, Interstellar, The Dark Knight*, and *Pirates of the Caribbean: At World's End*.

In fact, Zimmer was working on the compositions for *The Simpsons Movie* and *Pirates of the Caribbean* at the same time, but he was not put off. James L. Brooks told *The Hollywood Reporter* that Zimmer liked, "using all his creative juices at once… it was a unique challenge." One thing that Zimmer focused on was to "try and express the style of *The Simpsons* without wearing the audience out," therefore he used Elfman's original opening theme from the series, but did not want to "overuse it."

For the soundtrack, Zimmer created a theme for each family member. Homer's leitmotif was a major focus, and smaller themes were composed for Bart and Marge.

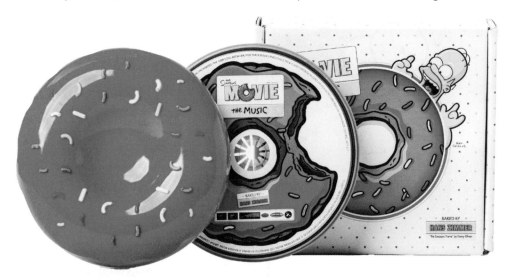

FUN FACT: THE LYRICS FOR "SPIDER PIG" WERE TRANSLATED FOR THE THIRTY-TWO DUBBED VERSIONS OF THE SONG WHEN THE FILM WAS RELEASED INTERNATIONALLY. THE SAME CHOIR LEARNED TO SING THE PIECE FOR EACH OF THE FOREIGN-LANGUAGE DUBS.

Closing Thoughts

To talk about *The Simpsons* merchandise and not talk about the music would be like watching *The Simpsons* without sound. Even though music merchandise is often disregarded as "gimmicky," the first couple of albums are among the rare pieces of merchandise that utilized the talents of the voice actors, composers, and writers to create an entirely new product outside of the show.

The album artworks were also mostly original, from the same illustrators who gave us the likes of *Simpsons Comics*. Therefore we got to see the family in whole new situations. I never thought I'd be faced with Bart Simpson's bare bottom when opening

The Yellow Album, let alone dressed in Ringo Starr's hat and jacket. Even the soundtrack albums, like *Testify*, had a considerable amount of thought go into their curation, with an entire booklet dedicated to the orchestra that gave us its iconic songs, alongside a commentary by Alf Clausen.

The albums were a product that expanded on *The Simpsons*'s world further than the edges of the TV screen. It bridged the gap between the show and the toys, T-shirts, and bubble bath, and the creators and characters that inspired them. It was merchandise that told us what Apu does when the Simpsons aren't around, and gave us beautifully animated fun music videos (ones that saw rare characters such as Jacques and Karl waltz in the streets). Even the later soundtrack albums gave us an appreciation for the music that truly made our favorite episodes' moments, as well as for the Simpsons themselves.

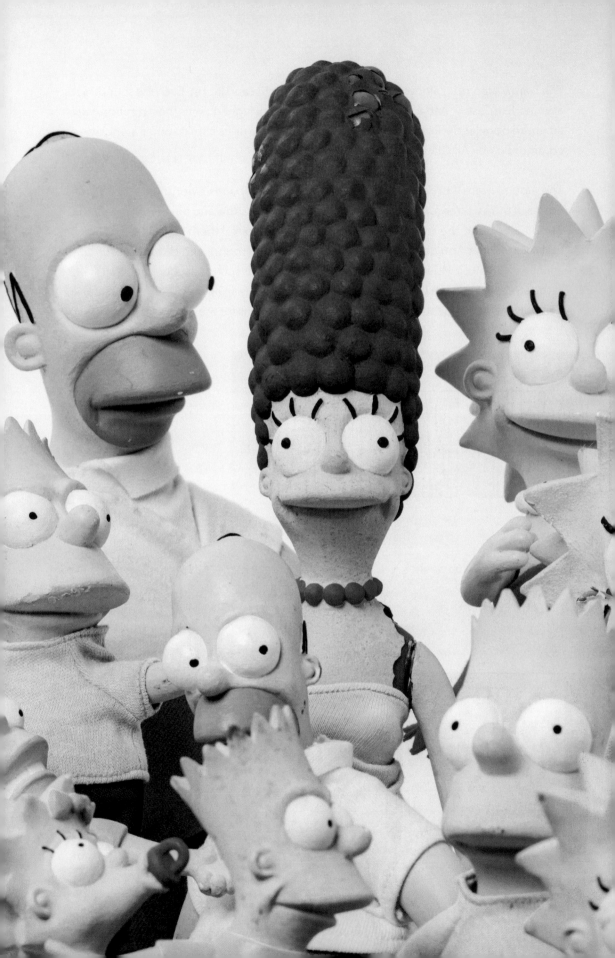

CHAPTER ELEVEN

Lost Toys

WARREN EVANS

Throughout the process of making this book, we realized on multiple occasions that including anywhere near everything was an impossible task. With that realization, some choices had to be made, and one of those choices was to spend some time focusing on the toys we don't remember, the toys that very few have seen, and that is because they don't *really* exist.

Over the course of producing merchandise, several toys don't make the cut and don't make it to final production. This leaves you with everything from a prototype to a paint master, all the way to a production sample. A production sample is the final step before production, and this is often the end of the road for a lot of toys. In the early days of the show, we saw this happen even more, due to uncertainty as to how long this little show would even last. Kinda funny to think about that now, huh?

As a collector, I'm always trying to dive deep and find out even more about lost toys, trying to put myself in the position of the person who decided to thumbs-down these items that were so close to the finish line. I think it's easy to toss our hands up and wonder why, but maybe they were right. Maybe the world wasn't ready for Baseball Bart or a Krusty rag doll. I guess we can't answer that now, but I have been lucky enough to track down some of these lost toys, along with some early stages of some not-so-lost toys. Let's take a look…

Sometime before this book was written, I participated in an auction made up mostly of these unreleased samples. The pieces I was able to win now make up some of my favorite and rarest pieces, but less because of the rarity and more because of that lingering question of, "Why weren't these made?"—I mean just look at Bart in that beach outfit!

With that in mind, I think it's also worth noting that in some cases, it really was as simple as a costume change. But in the case of the beach Bart in the above photo, he is significant for a few reasons. You see, DanDee made plenty of Barts, but not only did they pass on producing him in this outfit, they also abandoned this type of packaging for any of the smaller dolls. While it was essentially a smaller version of the packaging used for the large, talking Bart, I guess they ultimately decided it was less efficient. Most other versions of Bart in this size came in packaging more like the following Bartman:

In all honesty, this Bartman remains a great mystery, but I will explain him the best I can. While information on this is a bit all over the place, one thing we do know is that in other cases, certain toy lines licensed unproduced American toys to places like Argentina, where we see a few items often mistakenly called "bootlegs" when, in reality, they were legitimate products.

In the case of this Bartman, I believe we have another of those situations. While he looks like a DanDee product, he was produced by a company called CityToy, and features copyright information via a card on his chest. It is possible that he is based on a lost DanDee prototype, but also possible he's a unique product inspired by the normal doll. Either way, he is single-handedly the most bizarre product in my entire collection, with photos of another one being near impossible to find.

This Bartman, as well as the situation surrounding him, is actually fairly common. We talk a lot about the uncertainty of the longevity of the show, and as a result of that, a lot of smaller-run or unproduced toys weren't exactly cataloged or accounted for. You can almost hear someone saying, "Who would care about some canceled toy?" I will address this once the time machine is finished.

As we saw in the group photo, other products featuring Bartman were also scrapped. Let's take a better look at one of my favorites:

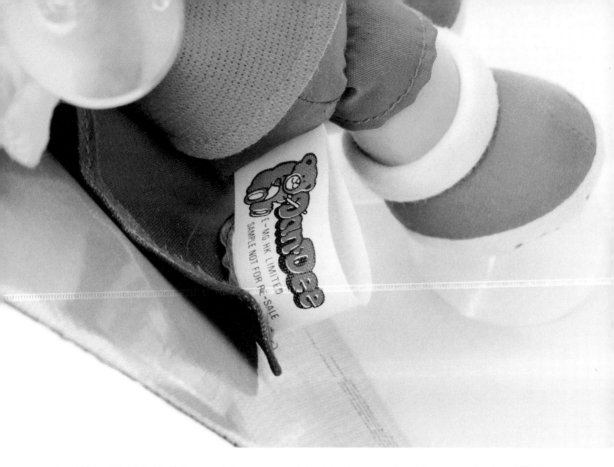

Luckily, with this doll, he has his name on his shirt, just so there is no confusion. While some people may not appreciate this unique, flat-faced style, they are actually some of my favorite products ever made. As I said back in the initial toy chapter, there is a special charm to these. Just look at that expression! This Bartman also features a sample tag on the packaging as well as the doll itself, even further proof that he wasn't produced beyond sample stage.

In addition to dolls like Bartman, we also saw lost versions from sub-lines within the main line. DanDee did a lot of Valentine's-Day-style dolls featuring the three Simpson children, but in this photo, we see a lost version of Bart next to a production sample of a Maggie that actually did make the cut. This Bart is also the only example from the entire line of a character without shoes on. Maybe that's why he failed?

But it wasn't just DanDee—other companies had toys that failed to pass the final approval. Mattel, for one, canceled an entire second wave of figures and products after releasing photos of them in a catalog. If you remember that Baseball Bart we talked about, he wasn't the only one. Let's look at that catalog…

COLLECTING THE SIMPSONS

Each figure has 5 sayings!

THE SIMPSONS™ FIGURE ASSORTMENT 📺

MATTEL, the master toy licensee for The Simpsons, is the one-stop shop for the best in Simpsons product. These poseable figures move at the neck, shoulders, waist, and hips. Each comes with its own accessory, a "word balloon" holder, and 5 interchangeable "word balloon" sayings. Great for collecting and trading. There's even room on the back of each "word balloon" for kids to write their own favorite sayings from the show! For ages 4 years and over. 11"H x 7½"W x 1¹³⁄₁₆"D Blister card.

9306 ASST. PAK 24

BASEBALL BART

NEW! A pitcher's worst nightmare! Bart yells his insulting digs from the dugout! He comes with a baseball bat and cap.

9306 ASST. PAK 24
9718 STD. PAK 12

9718 BASEBALL BART Figure

There was a time when I spent more time thinking about these toys than almost any *Simpsons* product. There is something to be said for how early it was, the fact that they were photographed, and just trying to tap into that unknowing feeling—the uncertainty of it all: Would the show last? Would a second wave of the toy line lose a lot of money for the company? I find myself getting lost in that idea. It's like looking back on a lost album or recording session, wondering how it would have impacted the very conversation we are having right now if they had made a different decision. This exact point is why we wanted to make this book.

But not all of these toys were "lost"—I guess it might be more accurate to say that in some cases they were "very sparingly distributed." Take this plate by Hamilton, for example:

Most people remember the other six designs—that to this day are pretty common—but when it comes to Bart and the Shark, an explanation as to its rarity is still not really there. Some people say it was canceled mid-production, and only a small batch were sold. Some people say it wasn't made at all, and that the only ones that exist are samples. Whatever the reason, this piece remains a very sought-after one for collectors. It's easily my favorite design from the series!

This also brings up an interesting point. It seems to me that *Simpsons* fans have always been very passionate. They've always looked for deeper meaning, wanted the episodes to fit even more tightly together than possible. And in most cases, those making the show truly loved it, but found that level of detail restrictive. They wanted to make every episode funny without having such a long list of connective tissue to follow. They probably didn't expect anyone to look that closely. A similar thing seems to be true of the merchandise. No one really thought to document the reasons why things weren't actually made, or why they are so hard to find–because as we noted earlier, I believe they just didn't think anyone would care about those details.

Well, here we are writing a book about it, so those notes would have been really helpful. I'm still thinking about that time machine…

Either way, I find myself inspired by the idea that there are still so many pieces we don't know about. There are so many great collectors still uncovering new connections and new hidden gems all the time, even as I write this. I spoke earlier about the many stages that lead to a toy being made, so let's look at an example:

For years I believed these to be prototypes, but I later learned that they were known
as the "paint master" stage of production. This comes before production samples,
and is rarely returned to the person who makes them, meaning they are often lost
or thrown away by the company. They remain among the best finds of my decade in
this hobby, and they really serve as a connection to a time and a place. I can't count
(because counting is hard) how many times I've used the word "charm" to describe
these early pieces, but just think about this: someone carved, sculpted, and painted
these characters that barely existed or mattered, over thirty years ago, only for us to
still be talking about them. I'm a big fan of that.

In a similar way, we will close out this chapter with what seems to be one of the lesser-seen sets of samples/prototypes. Some time ago, I was contacted about these by someone who only collected kites. (This is not a joke.) They had owned these for almost thirty years, and were looking to clear some space. Some of you may remember a Bart Simpson windsock called a "hang-around," but it seems that they originally planned on making more of them. Here is Homer and Marge…

This is an interesting situation where I am unsure just how many of these exist. Before this interaction, no one I know had ever heard of or seen them. In my research, I couldn't find any examples of packaging or other evidence to support these ever making it very far down the chain.

I'm confident there are enough items like this that we will be uncovering new ones for years to come. You could dedicate an entire second hobby to that research. An important mindset for me throughout this journey has been to assume there is so much I still don't know. That openness can only help, and it will certainly keep you from sounding like Comic Book Guy.

CHAPTER TWELVE

The Real
Simpsons
House

LYDIA HICKS

If there is a piece of *Simpsons* history that has always fascinated me, it is the construction of the real Simpsons house. Not only is its story one that could inspire a brilliant episode, but I believe that this marketing campaign helps track the shift from what I dub the "Simpsonsmania" of the '90s, to the approaching (and more turbulent) millennium for *The Simpsons*.

In 1997, fans were given the chance to win a life-sized replica of the Simpsons' house, and the details were immaculate. There were Duff cans in the fridge, Homer's car in the driveway, rows of the family's identical clothes in the closets, a peanut butter and jelly sandwich under Bart's bed, Lisa's sax, and, of course, Marge's corn cob curtains.

The Idea

Strangely, the idea for the build didn't come from *The Simpsons,* or even FOX, but Kaufman & Broad, a real estate development and construction company. Their new housing development in Nevada needed advertising, so they left it to their Head of Marketing, Jeff Charney, to devise a plan.

Jeff's plan? Give one lucky fan the chance to win 742 Evergreen Terrace (constructed by K&B) or $75,000.

You might think it would be difficult to get this campaign approved by FOX's licensing. *The Simpsons* was huge in the '90s, and having *The Simpsons* associated with you, or your company, pretty much guaranteed exposure, and exposure costs money.

But by 1997, the show's future seemed less certain with "Simpsonsmania" slowing down—a natural reaction caused by the settling of viewership combined with *The Simpsons* now sharing the TV schedule with a growing number of other adult animated shows. *King of the Hill, South Park,* and *Family Guy* were all created and aired around 1997 to 1998, and even though they were all obviously inspired by *The Simpsons,* the TV executives knew that they needed to ensure *The Simpsons* stayed on top. So K&B's house giveaway, with its national advertising potential, seemed to be a promotional vehicle that could help.

Design and Construction

Headed by Mike Woodley (project manager), Manny Gonzalez (architect), and Rick Floyd (production designer), the team pored over hundreds of episodes and storyboards loaned by FOX. The team was dedicated to constructing the most accurate layout of the home while balancing building regulations, such as the actual size of the house. The Simpsons house was originally calculated to be set across a fifty-foot plot, but Mike and Manny's forty-foot plot meant that the house had to be narrowed.

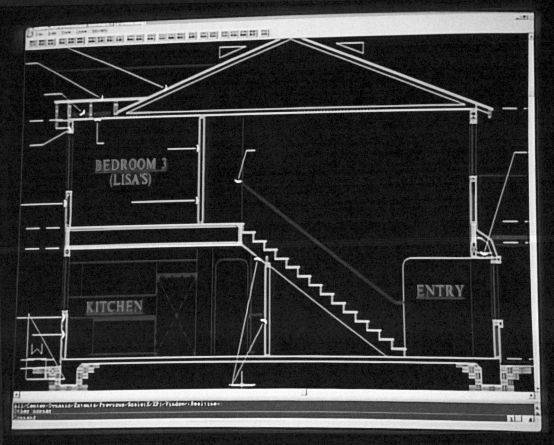

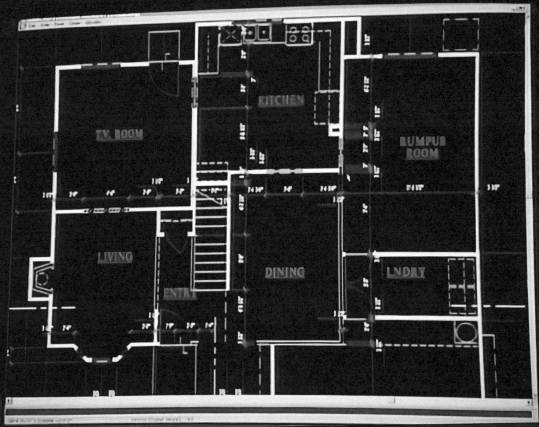

Otherwise, the team was given complete freedom when playing with cartoon continuity. So doors were widened and lengthened to accommodate Marge's hair and Homer's... broad physique, and the floors were poured and painted concrete to mimic the show's flat colors. Woodley also wanted to be conscious to balance this whimsy with functional features: "We knew someone had to live in it, so the kitchen was a little bigger than it is on the show... It had to be a real house."

Rick Floyd then added details for verisimilitude, purchasing over two thousand *Simpsons* knick-knacks for the home. He sourced items like the family's clothing, Lisa's saxophone, made mouse holes for the skirting boards, painted oil stains on the driveway, flagged down a car similar to Homer's (paying the bemused owner $700 for it), and even painted it pink. He spoke to the *LA Times* about this with specific reference to the food in Snowball II's bowl: "We picked the marshmallows that matched our color scheme out of a box of Lucky Charms and lacquered them together."

The house was quickly reaching a standard that would impress the critical eyes of Matt Groening, diehard *Simpsons* fans...and maybe, just maybe, Comic Book Guy.

Matt Groening Visits and Fan Reactions

Nearing the house's completion, FOX and K&B arranged tours for fans that proved hugely popular. In fact, a glimpse into the family's home drummed up two-hour wait times with a total of 500,000 visitors over this period. Fans were made to wear surgical-style boots to protect the flooring, and the house was generally treated with the utmost respect. But that's not to say that a few opportunists didn't decide to swipe some *Simpsons* swag, with Gonzalez mentioning that a lot of the decor had to be glued down.

Upon the house's completion, a party was held to celebrate. Matt Groening attended and was given the grand tour and the opportunity to leave his signature of approval. So, in graffiti, he wrote, "El Barto was here" on the garage wall before pressing his hands into the path's wet cement, literally solidifying the occasion. Along with him came Homer, Marge, Bart, Lisa, and Maggie themselves...albeit dressed in costumes that were slightly nightmare-inducing.

And the Winner Is...

By this point, the campaign had reached the ears of Pepsi, and they too joined FOX and K&B. It was a ballsy move considering that it was only one year earlier that Pepsi had "joked" about giving away a twenty-three-million-dollar fighter jet and gotten into some hot water. So, with their inclusion, the competition rules were established. All the participant needed to do was purchase Mug Root Beer, Brisk Iced Tea, or Slice and each can (or bottle) would have a number written on the label. If the number matched the one shown during the episode "The City of New York vs. Homer Simpson," then you were a winner!

TV adverts explaining the rules were shown across the US, notably on FOX Kids, presented by *Life With Louie*'s Louis Anderson. In these commercials, Anderson would wake up in the Simpsons house and explore it with awe and wonder. He would play Lisa's sax, fall down the stairs, and shout at Ned, and his family, to shut up.

Therefore, on September 21, 1997, *Simpsons* fans eagerly settled in to watch the season nine premiere, which saw Homer take the family to New York after Barney left his car illegally parked at the World Trade Center. It was all going to plan, the episode rolled, and then the winning number flashed on screen…

So who was the lucky winner? Months of planning, thousands of dollars spent, global exposure and…nothing happened. Whoever held the winning number (9786065) never stepped forward to claim their prize, and still hasn't to this day.

The organizers resorted to plan B, which was to draw a number from a raffle of fifteen million entries. And so, three months later, in December 1997, Mrs. Barbara Howard, a sixty-three-year-old retired factory worker from Kentucky, was declared the lucky winner.

Barbara lived in the rural and beautiful farmlands of Richmond, Kentucky, so much so that FOX's limo couldn't even make it down the dirt tracks to collect her. But they persevered and flew her out to Nevada on her first-ever plane ride. She loved gambling under the bright lights of Las Vegas, and was treated to a grand ceremony giving her the giant yellow key to her new home. However, it was during her interview with the *Las Vegas Sun* that some foreboding words emerged: "I gotta get down to earth again before I know what to do… I just want to gamble now."

So, like the neon lights of Vegas, Barbara's excitement about the house dimmed eventually, and she decided to take the $75,000 cash instead. Some were shocked, considering that the house held more value, but she was an elderly lady living a happy and quiet life, on a successful ostrich farm, with responsibilities and a family to look after. But she did offer a solution. "What I'd really like," she said in a telephone interview with the *LA Times*, "is to have Kaufman & Broad build me the house just like it is with everything in it, right here… I'd give anything to have it here and have people go through and pay a small fee that would go to the cancer fund. My brother has cancer." Sadly, this request was never accepted.

What Happened to the House?

Unfortunately, this gave the house a blunt ending. The option to keep it open for tours was impossible, due to housing regulations, and the homeowner's association demanded that the external bright, cartoon colors be stripped and drowned in shades of beige to blend in with its neighbors.

Lonely old 742 Evergreen Terrace was soon lost and forgotten in the dusty deserts of Nevada, painted the boring colors of the dirt it was built upon, it became a burden. Matt Groening even flirted with the idea of blowing it up live on TV. This disrespect only spiraled with an increase in looting and ransacking of its furnishings. Portraits were torn off the walls, props were stolen…this wasn't just a "four-finger discount, dude"—it was heartbreaking.

The only other solution was to sell the house as it was, and even though K&B attempted to give it somewhat of a facelift, it didn't help attract potential buyers. However, after four long years of an empty, lonely existence, the Simpsons house was finally saved in 2001.

Danielle, a secretary for K&B, bought the house almost blindly, having practically forgotten its history. To her, this house was simply a bargain buy, and one she could turn into a family home.

The family became the first, and only, residents of the house. Upon moving in, they discovered that, while the exterior was as bland as a biscuit, they described the interiors as "a giant Crayola box," with other strange design choices including cupboards that opened into brick walls. Danielle also mentioned that she regularly receives hilarious mail addressed to the actual Simpsons family: letters addressed to Homer from the Salvation Army, shampoo samples for Marge, and even a flyer from PetSmart for Santa's Little Helper.

But there were certainly other "oddities" that came with the house beyond decor and mail…*Simpsons* fans.

Purchasing such an iconic home linked Danielle with the *Simpsons* fandom. So fans descended upon it to steal trees, photograph it profusely, and knock on the front door at all hours. The family even recalled one story where a man planted himself on the doorstep, clutching a huge stuffed animal, and stared at the door for a long period of time. In fact, fans still invade this poor family's privacy to this day, feeling somewhat of an ownership over it just because they are fans of the show.

SPEAKING OF WHICH, I WOULD LIKE TO TAKE THIS OPPORTUNITY TO REMIND FANS THAT THIS IS A FAMILY HOME. THEREFORE, I WOULD SUGGEST THAT, DESPITE OUR EXCITEMENT AND CURIOSITY, WE REFRAIN FROM BOTHERING THE PEOPLE WHO LIVE THERE BY KNOCKING ON THEIR DOOR.

CHAPTER TWELVE: THE REAL SIMPSONS HOUSE

The Underlying Importance of the Simpsons House

The project was an incredible marketing campaign, but it goes further than that—it's a chapter in *Simpsons* history. Building the house was done at a time when there was a real change in the market for *The Simpsons* in both its merchandise and place on TV. As discussed, in 1997, the show's future was less certain. The *LA Times* reported that sales of tie-in *Simpsons* merchandise had fallen off from its high, with the number of companies producing *Simpsons* goods dropping by 75 percent. The house competition came at a time when FOX really felt they needed a promotional vehicle to keep *The Simpsons* ahead to compete against the growing number of TV animated shows. But did it work?

While I do not believe that this marketing campaign can be credited with the success of *The Simpsons* on any scale—in fact I think it's a *product* of its success—there is no denying that the show maintained its title as the world's favorite cartoon family longer than anyone ever expected during this time. Even now, *The Simpsons* has been named the most successful series on its platform, Disney+, and I think it is a credit to the makers and the magic of the show, as well as to us fans who continue to cheer it on.

What the Simpsons house proved was just how large, loyal, and dedicated the fan base was. There is no other show where I can imagine 500,000 people queuing around the block, in the outskirts of Nevada, just for a peek into an otherwise "typical American home," even if it was on television. It speaks volumes that the show's own creator was willing to blow the house up, but the fans were willing to fight tooth and nail just for a small piece of decor. But *Simpsons* fans have a loyalty and dedication like those of no other TV animated show. Whether you used to watch the show, or still do, I am sure there is still an underlying respect for the doors this family opened in their genre.

CHAPTER THIRTEEN

Universal Studios

LYDIA HICKS

It was always a dream of mine to visit Springfield. I remember being nine years old finishing off a school project which was to design our very own imaginary towns out of household junk. Some kids made intricate little metropolises, and one kid even got their dad to build a working railway. So when I presented mine to the class—an upturned-egg-carton town painted with layers of peeling acrylic paint, PVA glue, and little character printouts—I was shocked that it was my little Springfield that the kids flocked to.

My project certainly wasn't original or imaginary, but it was a clumsy way of recreating a town I was so keen to be a part of. My friends and I would point at the warped boxes while shouting, "There's Moe's!" or "Ooo look, Snake's robbing Apu again." Who knew that in a few years, instead of looking down at a miniature town, I would be looking up and absorbing the world of Springfield for real at Universal Studios Springfield, USA: Home of The Simpsons.

So, let's talk about the making of Springfield at Universal Studios: a place where you can enjoy a Duff at Moe's, cause nuclear meltdowns, answer prank calls from Bart Simpson, and even help yourself to a donut as big as your head. The land also has exclusive merchandise that you can buy (or win) and is able to fully submerge you into the sounds, thrills, and adventures of *The Simpsons* through…the Simpsons Ride!

The Simpsons Ride

From 1991 to 2007, the space where the Simpsons Ride now sits housed Back to the Future: The Ride. This immersive simulator took you through a four-minute adventure, literally back to the future. But by the 2000s, Universal Studios wanted to update the area, and in mid-2006, rumors began surfacing about when the ride would close and which franchise would replace it. The two choices were *The Simpsons* and *Fast & Furious*. And even though the latter was (and still is) Universal's biggest hit, *The Simpsons* was selected because of its broader appeal.

So, after thrilling the minds and imaginations of fans for sixteen years, the DeLorean made one final trip back in time in September 2007, before flying off into the clouds forever… leaving *The Simpsons* to swoop in as harmoniously as its opening credits.

Building the Ride

Constructing the Simpsons ride started only two years before it opened, helped along by the fact that the skeleton and mechanics were all reused from the *Back to the Future* ride. Universal Studios then went to Matt Groening, executive producer Al Jean and a team of longtime writers including Matt Selman and Matt Warburton to create the ride's plot.

Warburton, writer of episodes such as "Springfield Up" and "Papa's Got a Brand New Badge," thought of the ride's core idea: Krusty the Clown is opening up a dangerous new theme park and, along with the family, he wants you to test-drive it!

He was inspired by a short story by Steven Millhauser where a man creates a theme park so dangerous that it starts to kill people. This was in keeping with Krusty's reputation, from his razorblade cereal to the horrors of Kamp Krusty (as well as his oh-so-willingness to slap his brand of approval sticker on any piece of dangerous junk...as long as they paid him enough).

This fatal fantasy funland was entitled Krustyland, a name first mentioned in season six's "'Round Springfield," where Krustyland's House of Knives ultimately decapitated tourists.

In my interview with Matt Selman, he explained: "Universal had a rough draft of what the 'plot' was for the ride, which took the form of a CGI animatic. The *Simpsons* team took some elements of that and reworked it into a new story. I feel like when we came on board we worked to emphasize the idea that this ride, in addition to being fun, would be a satire of theme parks themselves. Universal didn't immediately love the idea that we were parodying theme park rides and the theme park experience, but since this was *The Simpsons* they eventually trusted us to make the ride actually funny."

The idea that the area was going to satirize theme parks in general was applied to everything: the gift shops, eateries, carnival games and hidden Easter eggs with quippy references – perfect for a show that is famous for parodying the real world.

FUN FACT: THE RIDE'S STATS: THE RIDE COST $40,000,000, HAS TWO NINETY-FOOT-TALL DOMED SCREENS, CAN ENTERTAIN ALMOST TWO THOUSAND GUESTS PER HOUR AND HAS FOUR SONY DIGITAL MOVIE PROJECTORS (AT SIXTY FRAMES PER SECOND) PER DOME!

The Grand Opening

On May 15, 2008, the Simpsons Ride was unveiled in Orlando, and only a few days later in Hollywood. Both events were huge, with Bill Davis, the President of Universal Orlando Resort, sporting a lovely Marge bouffant along with a few hundred other guests. The Simpsons family attended, in their costumes, accompanied with a brass band. The ceremony in Hollywood even had a man getting blasted out of a cannon, pyrotechnics, Matt Groening, and supervillain Sideshow Bob himself, Kelsey Grammer.

The ride was a huge success praised for its hilarity and satire. *Theme Park Insider* gave its stamp of approval, labeling the Simpsons Ride the "Best New Theme Park Attraction" worldwide in 2008.

FUN FACT: UNIVERSAL ORLANDO HOSTED THE SIMPSON RIDE'S ONE-MILLIONTH RIDER ON JULY 14, 2008, REACHING THE MILESTONE FASTER THAN ANY OTHER ATTRACTION IN THE RESORT!

Expanding the Park

Although the Simpsons Ride opened on May 15, 2008, the land of Springfield was still being developed. Soon the Back to the Future gift shops were replaced by Apu's Kwik-E-Mart (the *Simpsons* parody of 7-Eleven stores) but instead of selling Apu's questionable hot dogs, it sells less harmful Simpsons merchandise.

In 2013, Universal Orlando's expansion of Springfield meant that the International Food & Film Festival was demolished to make way for Fast Food Boulevard. This introduced the likes of Krusty Burger, The Frying Dutchman, Duff Gardens, Lard Lad Donuts, and Bumblebee Man's Taco Truck.

It was also around this time that the carnival games were introduced in front of the Simpsons Ride, as well as Kang and Kodos's Twirl 'n' Hurl. This Aero Top Jet ride paid homage to the iconic Treehouse of Horror aliens with sharp teeth and an uncontrollable drooling problem. As a guest, you would be in a flying saucer that reached speeds of up to 1/51,595,995 the speed of light (a.k.a., 13 m.p.h.), enough to lift it to take you ten breathtaking feet above the earth!

Hollywood's main Springfield expansion happened on May 23, 2015, with the remodeling of Doc Brown's Fried Chicken to turn it into Cletus' Chicken Shack, and the inclusion of Springfield Elementary, the Android's Dungeon, the Aztec Theater, Springfield Penitentiary, Herman's Military Antiques, and Springfield's Police Department.

COLLECTING THE SIMPSONS

FUN FACT: DID YOU KNOW THAT UNIVERSAL STUDIOS HOLLYWOOD HAS SERVED CHICKEN IN THE SAME LOCATION SINCE 1915? THE ORIGINAL NAME WAS THE FLOWER DRUM RESTAURANT, AND IT WAS PART OF UNIVERSAL FOUNDER CARL LAEMMLE'S UNIVERSAL CITY! THAT RESTAURANT WAS THEN REPLACED BY DOC BROWN'S CHICKEN, WHICH IS NOW, OF COURSE, CLETUS' CHICKEN SHACK. THIS COULD BE WHY UNIVERSAL WAS SO ADAMANT ABOUT KEEPING THE BUILDING A CHICKEN SHOP—TO MAINTAIN ITS CLUCKIN' LEGACY.

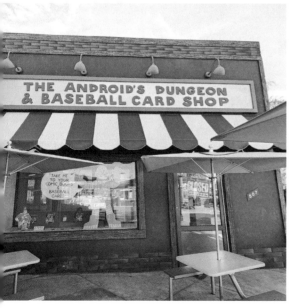

Everything You Can Do in Springfield!

Walking through the town of Springfield is a credit to how well Universal does theming. It is designed with the bright bubblegum palette of the show, embedded with references and is soundtracked with *The Simpsons* musical score playing throughout the area. You can also try an abundance of food, drink and treats inspired by the show.

Trying to spot every tiny detail in recreating Springfield will make your head spin. There's The Android's Dungeon & Baseball Card Shop, owned by Comic Book Guy, on your right, and the town square's statue of Jebediah Springfield on your left. There's also a bar tributing Duff Gardens outside, looking over Universal's lake, with all seven Duff mascots. In the Hollywood park, there's also an interactive button for you to press that causes a nuclear meltdown!

Krusty's Carnival Games

Lining the front of the Simpsons Ride are traditional carnival games with a "*Simpsons* edge." The classic Ring Toss is called "Mr. Burns's Radioactive Rings," with green-glowing nuclear "rods." There is the Whack-A-Mole game featuring Itchy and Scratchy, as well as Dunk the Flunk—a take on the classic basketball-hoop toss where you can win your own Principal Skinner or Groundskeeper Willie. Interestingly, a lot of the merchandise given away as prizes can only be obtained by winning and is not sold publicly.

The Simpsons's idea of satirizing theme parks is carried over into this area with blatant warning signs to customers, such as, "You can't do it! Don't even try!"

Drown Your Sorrows at Moe's Tavern

Never before would I have thought that I could sit on a bar stool and sip a cold glass of Duff while pouring my problems out to a moody bartender…well, you can (except for the last point—the bartender was far too chipper to be Moe).

Moe's Tavern is a faithful recreation of the downscale joint, complete with cartoonish, purple-hued molding and orange and green stained glass. Inside, you'll find all kinds of *Simpsons* references, such as an interactive phone to answer Bart's prank calls, the love-tester, and various photos of the bar regulars. You can also meet the notorious Barney Gumble, the only Springfield resident who loves beer more than Homer Simpson.

If you would like to challenge the bar-fly, you can purchase Duff Beer here. Duff at Universal is an American-style amber lager with roasted malt and hints of caramel, and it's at this location that you can also order the famous Flaming Moe!

The Kwik-E-Mart

Peruse the Kwik-E-Mart without fear of being held hostage by Snake, or entrapped by a refrigerator like poor Jasper. This gift shop will satisfy all of your *Simpsons* merchandising needs, from Bart-head sippers, Homer slippers, rails of shirts, Kang and Kodos plushies, and rows and rows of "Bort" merch!

There's also a wide variety of *Simpsons*-themed snacks, like Farmer Billy's Choco-Bacon-Bar (from season fifteen's "Simple Simpson"), Bobo's Gummy Bears (from season five's "Rosebud"), and Krusty Klump Bars. All are packaged in quintessentially *Simpsons* wrapping smothered in references that both the casual and hardcore fan will appreciate.

From floor to ceiling there are promotional posters for in-universe products such as Chef Lonely Hearts Soup for One, Krusty-O's, Much Ado About Stuffing, and Squishees. Again we are met by more blatant and satirical theme park signage such as, "These things won't buy themselves" or "Just browsing? Just leave!"

Mmmm... Food

At Universal, Springfield is the place for food. You have Krusty Burger, Cletus' Chicken Shack, Lisa's Teahouse of Horror (offering healthy alternatives), The Frying Dutchman, and Luigi's Pizza. Outside the food court is Bumblebee Man's Taco Truck as well as Lard Lad's Donuts at its own kiosk. Here you can buy the Big Pink as well as Springfield's Flavors of the Day, Chocolate Glazed, Maple Bacon, Froot Loops…and more…mmm… more donuts.

Hollywood's Secret Krusty Hall of Fame

Every inch of Springfield's Fast-Food Boulevard is stuffed with *Simpsons* references and gags that provide special treats for fans of the long-running show. However, in the Hollywood park specifically, you may not know that there's an entire secret room upstairs in Krusty Burger that is full of Easter eggs. What started out as a pretty plain room has slowly transformed into a museum to commemorate Krusty's huge achievements. What makes this room even more special is the illustrations slotted between the memorabilia; these are drawings of various beloved one-time characters drawn by animators and artists from the actual show in their own unique and individual styles.

A Legacy: Universal Studios Springfield, USA

Universal Studios Springfield, USA: Home of The Simpsons remains as popular as ever as it wows the imaginations of guests every single day. Even the Simpsons family themselves got to visit the park in season twenty-three's "The Food Wife"!

It remains a place that marks all that *The Simpsons* has achieved, and is the closest any one of us could get to the actual world it created. The area is important to the cast and crew of the show too, using it as a venue to mark their special events such as the release of "Treehouse of Horror XXXIII." This was a horror special widely, and critically, acclaimed for its experimentation in the anime-sphere, as well as its parody of *Westworld*. And its episodes like this that continually prove that *The Simpsons* still certainly has a space on TV, but also at Universal Studios.

However, even if Springfield's existence can't live forever in the parks, its legacy will. *The Simpsons* and Springfield opened up a world just like our own, but wildly more colorful, and wildly more fun - this made it all the more "Universal-ly" loved. From grumpy old Dad, who just wants to sit and sip a beer, to the wide-eyed kids with donut frosting around their mouths dragging Mom to try out Krusty's "Thrilltacular, Upsy-downsy, Spins-aroundsy, Teen-operated Thrill Ride" just one more time…they promise!

CHAPTER FOURTEEN

How to Start a Collection

WARREN EVANS

It wouldn't be much of a book about collecting if we didn't really dig into what collecting means to me, as well as what it means to collect for yourself…and what I think is the best way to approach the hobby.

To me, collecting anything really taps into some unknown sense of preservation and admiration. Obviously you might not always "admire" the subject of your collection, but I think with most people, it stems from a profound admiration of all the things a property can mean to someone. I myself admire what *The Simpsons* has meant to so many people, and the merchandise is a direct, tangible extension of that.

There is something to be said for anyone who takes the time to build the equivalent of a shrine in their home. I'm not sure if we do it because it's fun to track stuff down, or because it's fun to buy things, or if it's just fun to scare people the first time they come over for dinner. All I do know is that when we collect toys, or bathroom products, or anything we've shown in this book, we are literally preserving it. We are locking a memory safely away in a glass case for people to continue to appreciate. This idea is exactly why we have museums, although those might be slightly more important. I'll let you all decide that for yourselves.

I'll get into how to start a collection, but first, I'll tell you how I got into it.

When I was a kid, I always enjoyed compiling or collecting in some way. I was obsessed with basketball, and a new pack of cards would make my entire weekend. I would spend hours organizing them in my binder. First I would put them in actual order, then I would organize by team, then I would organize them by player, then by player and team... I think you understand where this is going. It took up a great deal of my time, and I felt accomplished with each new order.

As time went on, I had less time for stuff as tedious as basketball cards, and moved on to things like comics, but in this case I cared less about condition, and more about the story and getting to the next one. To me, the parallel of these two things sort of explains a lot about who I am and the way I think about collecting now. I think everyone needs a little bit of both to fully understand the passion behind something as time-consuming as completing multiple toy lines all at the same time.

I moved on from comics eventually, and didn't really collect anything for over a decade. I spent more time playing video games and writing music, things that required way less space, but I also think that contributed to the way collecting grabbed me. Once I was traveling less, settling down a little more, the idea of focusing on something like a collection became very appealing. But I don't think you can ever fully plan where a collection will go. Part of why it is so special is the organic nature of collecting. It's the fact that each new item changes the collection, broadens your interest within it, and can sometimes change your focus. Being open to that is key, in my opinion.

For me, *Simpsons* collecting started very small. My girlfriend, now wife, had never really seen *The Simpsons*. She obviously knew what it was, but had never really dug in or spent time with it. Now, it's important to mention here that at the time, I was also buying a fair amount of VHS tapes—something I enjoyed hunting for a while—and one day I stumbled across a few volumes of the "Best of" collection of *The Simpsons* on VHS, the same ones featured both on the cover and earlier in this book. I thought these volumes would be a fun way to introduce her more to the show, and I still believe that they were. We didn't have as many options to watch the show at the time, other than the DVD sets after all, and who doesn't love rewinding?

A significant thing happened that day: something about the packaging really dug itself into my brain, and I immediately hopped on eBay to find more of the volumes. Before I knew it, I had them all. Then I found a Bart plush here or a Bart pin there, then a friend would send me a photo of a Homer toy he saw and ask if I needed it. (Thanks, Lars.) Then I'd find a Lisa doll at the flea market, a Homer shirt at a thrift store. Once again, I think you see where this is going. Each little piece took me deeper and deeper down the rabbit hole.

So, as you can read, collecting really did begin in a very natural way for me, and it really took hold of my spare time and spare brain space. It quickly went from a small shelf in my closet, to a plastic tub under the bed, and suddenly our apartment was too small for my new hobby, so we got a house. This new hobby became somewhat of a driving force for some other big life decisions, and I'd make them all again, because I'm sitting here writing a chapter about it, in a book full of photos of my stuff.

But I also think it's important to note that collecting is not for everyone, and I think that has become more clear to me over the last decade. Having this many things can be easily overwhelming, and finding space for new additions can really eat up your weekend. That is the exact moment when you realize the hobby is a labor of love, and not always an easy one—but usually a great one, as long as you have the patience. And even if sometimes you don't, it's okay to let yourself off the hook, allow your relationship with the hobby to shift in different directions as time goes on. Remember, this is about you!

I mentioned earlier that "There is no wrong way to collect." When I say this, I'm essentially saying that there are no rules. There is no correct way to start, whether it's an accident, or you are deciding as you read this book. You will encounter people who feel a sense of ownership of this hobby, out of their own passion or self-given expertise, but that's just part of their own journey. As my good friend Kane Gordon always says, "Freak what you feel."

Some people might yell at you for opening that rare watch, or displaying that set of figures "loose" rather than keeping them in their original packaging. As for me, I think it is extremely important to let the collection exist in whatever way brings you the most joy. If opening figures not only saves you room, but brings you more joy, rip that packaging to shreds! If you're the kind of person who likes to keep records in the shrink, then feel free to keep your toys safely tucked away inside their boxes. I fully endorse and support both approaches, and anyone who doesn't might be collecting for the wrong reasons.

You also might find that some people collect because they enjoy owning things with value. I also don't think this is wrong, but I also believe value too often overshadows actual feeling. If you like a toy more because it's valuable than because it makes you smile, how much is that toy really worth? This is another key point that I tried to lock in early on. We all love knowing something we own has monetary value, but I believe that should come second to emotional value. The kind of value that reminds us of the good side of life. Is that too deep? Let's move on.

So what's the best way to start a collection? First and foremost, it's important to have areas of focus. Maybe you saw someone's World of Springfield toys and that really sparked your interest…maybe you found a nice Applause plush at your local thrift store and something clicked inside your brain like it did with mine. In situations like this, it can be super overwhelming to just look for anything with *The Simpsons* on it, because as we have laid out in this book, that is extremely broad. So it helps early on to decide where you want to start,. This will allow you to get the ball rolling without sending you

in a million different directions. And following that, you will find more natural launching pads into other lines and types of collectibles.

I used to tell people all the time to "Decide what you really like," and I still think this is good advice. In my early days, I thought I liked it all, and I probably wasted a lot of time finding stuff that I liked less than other stuff. I didn't start collecting with some goal of having the biggest collection in the world, and I think if I had, I'd love it a lot less now. Realizing that really freed me in a way, and that's when I started dialing in my areas of focus. This calls back to that emotional value I spoke of.

If you have followed me online for any amount of time, you know I have a soft spot for ceramics from the UK and France. Somewhere in the first few years, this became a large area of focus for me. I've spent a lot of my time as a collector so far hunting down a very select few items, and I only appreciate them more as a result. Think of it as a way of not feeling obligated to buy every *Simpsons* thing you see, a way to remind yourself it's a marathon and not a race. To use another record analogy, maybe you'd rather find a special record rather than browse the three-for-five-dollars bin.

With that said, to all my three-for-five-dollars people—I love you. Maybe being particular isn't your thing, and that's more than okay. I think a lot of collectors start this way, and I'm sure some people prefer it. This can also give you plenty of options for future trades or to sell. As I write this, it occurs to me that this is actually another part of what is so beautiful about the hobby. You can laser in, or you can go with the flow. It's all about finding what works best for you and your budget, as well as what brings you joy. At the end of the day, we do this for joy, right? I really want to hammer this point home. "Sorry to repeat myself, but it'll help you remember."

So what about the best way to find stuff? In my early years, I found tons of stuff out and about, in the real world. Unfortunately, this has gotten much more difficult for a few reasons. As with all vintage markets, this has become a little more competitive. Everyone wants to find that Bart doll for two dollars and sell it for thirty, and this can all drive the market in all kinds of directions. One of the major downsides of buying online now is how easy it is for people to use the wrong metrics to inflate prices.

If I can give one major piece of advice for collectors who buy online: make sure you use sold listings to gauge value. Those fifteen available listings aren't really the best way to know what it's worth. The only true way to do that is to see what people are actually willing to pay via sold listings. Sometimes want outweighs price, and I'm as guilty as anyone, but just make sure you keep your eyes peeled as you begin this hobby. Otherwise, your wallet will take quite a beating.

In reality, I meet people more often than I'd expect who seem intimidated by the thought of buying online for this exact reason. It's also possible they just don't like waiting. (I'm that lady from the meme who sits next to the mailbox.) What I will say is that only finding stuff in person will add decades to your collection journey, especially if your interests grow outside of just products made in the USA. So just be careful, and I think you'll adjust in no time.

I'm not even sure I've properly explained how to start a collection, because I don't think anyone can do that. I just hope you take something away from my advice. The concept of collecting can be such an interesting one, with a lot of layers. Maybe you've fallen out of love with the hobby, and you can't figure out why. Maybe you've just recently worked up the courage or finalized your plan to start a collection for the first time. Maybe you spent years with this hobby and then sold it and now you feel regret. And maybe, maybe you think collecting is strange and you're reading this as part of some research paper. I think all of these things are great reasons to read this book. (I also get paid!)

When it comes to anything I like, I try to always make sure people understand that I don't consider myself an expert. Sometimes I am weary of praise, because I truly believe the road to the most happiness is knowledge and a willingness to be wrong. What I find value in might mean nothing to the next person, and even less to the next person. This is why I believe sharing knowledge and learning through experience is one of the most rewarding things in this life.

So with that, I will wish you the best of luck on your journey either down, back to, or away from the rabbit hole. Either we are glad to have you, or we will miss you.

Find joy!

Conclusion

When the three of us started writing this book, there was one thing we all wanted to do: celebrate *The Simpsons*.

James, Lydia, and Warren were all children who loved a cartoon. But it was a love that never ended, and naturally, when you love something so much, you want to preserve it. Warren's collection, Lydia and James's YouTube channels, and *this book* is a vessel for that preservation, a space for us to indulge in the legacy of *The Simpsons* as the self-proclaimed "Simpsons Historians" (or nerds) that we are.

There is no denying that there are those more qualified to write about the making of the show. So we felt it important to write a book from our own perspective, a consumer perspective, to focus on *The Simpsons*'s cultural impact and how it affected merchandise.

There was the family's explosion in success, where merchandise was mass-produced even before the first episode. The "Bartmania" in the '90s that got school kids wearing Bart Simpson T-shirts as a prepubescent and political act of self-expression, as well as the show's adaptation to suit the development of home entertainment technology—which, unfortunately, came at the expense of *Simpsons* fans' incomplete DVD collections.

To quote another animated show, *South Park*, "Simpsons Did It." Episode plots, characters, jokes, and merchandise, *The Simpsons* creators are pioneers in "doing it all." And it was its abundance of merchandise that made it the most addictive entity to collect. Therefore, when writing this book, we knew right away that there was no way we could cover every piece of merchandise, but could rather show you the scope of how far it reaches. We shed light on the stranger corners of collecting, without you having to scour garage sales or burn a hole in your pocket.

So we are sorry to say, our curious collector, that your thrift-shop-searching days are not quite over, there are more *Simpsons* artifacts to be discovered and treasured, whether it be a little Maggie plushy, a Lisa Simpson first aid kit, or even a Bart Simpson T-shirt that will take you back to being the little rebel you always wanted to be. The world of *The Simpsons* is endless, and isn't that why we love it?

We sincerely hope that we have embiggened your mind and knowledge. But if you would like to continue learning with us, you can join Lydia and James on YouTube by subscribing to *The Simpsons Theory*. You can also listen to Warren's "Simpsons Is Greater Than…" podcast, and keep up to date with all of his latest treasures by following @bartofdarkness on Instagram.

Lydia, James, and Warren

About the Authors

Warren Evans (Bart of Darkness) is the creator and owner of one of the most prolific *Simpsons* fan and collector pages around. He fosters an extensive online community, details his massive collection of rare memorabilia, and highlights some of the best moments and episodes *The Simpsons* have to offer. He also has a podcast called "Simpsons is Greater Than..." where he expands on the cultural impact of *The Simpsons* as well as conversations with cast and crew from all eras of *The Simpsons*.

Together, **Lydia Hicks** and **James Hicks** created *The Simpsons Theory*, the largest YouTube channel dedicated to *The Simpsons*. Over their careers, they have interviewed writers, showrunners, animators, and artists of the show to produce videos to educate and entertain *Simpsons* fans around the world.

The duo discuss the most poignant moments in the show's history, piece together in-depth character timelines, and are well-known for their series, *The Treehouse of Horror Kill Count*. They also wrote the book *The Simpsons Secret: A Cromulent Guide to How The Simpsons Predicted Everything*, and have even been rumored to appear in an episode of *The Simpsons*!

Mango Publishing, established in 2014, publishes an eclectic list of books by diverse authors—both new and established voices—on topics ranging from business, personal growth, women's empowerment, LGBTQ studies, health, and spirituality to history, popular culture, time management, decluttering, lifestyle, mental wellness, aging, and sustainable living. We were named 2019 *and* 2020's #1 fastest growing independent publisher by *Publishers Weekly*. Our success is driven by our main goal, which is to publish high quality books that will entertain readers as well as make a positive difference in their lives.

Our readers are our most important resource; we value your input, suggestions, and ideas. We'd love to hear from you—after all, we are publishing books for you!

Please stay in touch with us and follow us at:

Facebook: Mango Publishing
Twitter: @MangoPublishing
Instagram: @MangoPublishing
LinkedIn: Mango Publishing
Pinterest: Mango Publishing
Newsletter: mangopublishinggroup.com/newsletter

Join us on Mango's journey to reinvent publishing, one book at a time.